Memoirs of my life

Kiri Atawhai Dewes

Published by

Heart Space Publications
PO Box 1085
Daylesford
Victoria
3460
Australia
Tel +61 450260348
www.heartspacebooks.com
pat@heartspacebooks.com

Copyright © 2020 Kiri Atawhai Dewes

All rights reserved under international copyright conventions. No part of this book may be reproduced, stored in a retrieval system, or transmitted in any form or by any means electronic, mechanical, photocopying, recorded or otherwise without written permission from Heartspace Publications.

Whilst every care has been taken to check the accuracy of the information in this book, the publisher cannot be held responsible for any errors, omissions or originality.
Published in 2020 at Melbourne

ISBN 9780-6489-21516

TESTIMONIALS

What a privilege it is to write about Aunty Kiri. For over the three decades she has been in my life. Aunty Kiri has been a role model for many communities and me, as she holds herself with integrity and care for all. I have seen her weep with a mourning mother, laugh with a young graduating person, and give public talks about her culture, her relationship to land and country, and how to strengthen youth through language and embracing heritage. I have been awed at times when her small physical stature can hold audiences in the palm of her hand by sharing her poems, her experiences, and her spirit with all peoples. I look forward to reading Aunty Kiri's book – I anticipate it will be funny, inspiring, but mostly healing as she shares her resilience and aroha with her readers.

Professor Kerrie Doyle Peita, PhD.

I have nothing but complete respect for Kiri Dewes. Not only does she impart amazing knowledge and wisdom, but does so in such a sharing and down to earth way. Often having people in fits of laughter, while imparting serious pearls of wisdom in such an uplifting way. Over the years she has been an inspiration, to not only the Maori people, but also the wider community. When traveling with her to NZ over the years, I have seen the deep respect, which has been shown to her by the local community, for her outstanding commitment to their culture and the younger generations. I am proud and thankful for our long lasting friendship.

Judy O'Donnell; Owner/Director Sacred Site Travel

The Wit and Wisdom of Kiri has inspired people in all walks of life. Her life story will amaze and amuse, it will inspire and lift. Kiri now in her 80's, is still inspiring and lifting people, especially young Maoris' helping them to keep their heritage, and to cope in their lives! A truly gifted poet, there is no end to her talents. Kiri is also the founder of Australia's Counsel of 13 Grandmothers, a huge honour to bring wisdom to all who listen!

Some of the 13 grandmothers

Grandmother Sue; Vortex Healing Centre

Acknowledgements

I wish to thank Maori Broadcasting, for the borrowing of my words from their 2009 documentary of my life story. I thank Jane Crisp for the use of her image for my cover.

DEDICATION

I dedicate this book to my five children - Wayne, Patrick, Judy, Shelley Rose and Christine; my grandchildren, great grandchildren and great, great grandchildren, with love.

A NOTE FROM THE PUBLISHER

The first time I arrived at Kiri's house, on rounding the corner, I heard a series of high-pitched cackles – full of mirth and joy. They suggested that the owner of the voice was a happy person. As I was to getting to know Kiri better, and as we poured over Kiri's writing – which was also pouring over her life – I could see that Kiri is filled with joy. I stayed at Kiri's house whilst we worked and always enjoyed my time there. When I came in that first time, she said, "Make this your home", and she meant it.

I was taken in by her large family, which at times seemed like a small nation, and made to feel part of that family. Across the ditch in New Zealand, it was the same, with great hospitality.

I had met Kiri several times before putting the book together and could not say I knew her, but through this book, Kiri and I became friends. How could we not? Kiri is Kiri – unique, intelligent, and funny – always funny. We spent many days together, where, in fits and starts, the book emerged. I have never had such fun producing a book.

No matter what is going on in your life,
give anyway.

Choose the mountain you want to cling to wisely.

Kiri is gruff and warm at the same time, which all my writing friends would say is an oxymoron. Her face will hold you in a glare as she pins you with her eyes – then, as if the sun emerges from a dark cloud, her smile lights up her face... She has a big heart, big enough to drive a truck into, yet she will growl at you at the same time. Her generosity of spirit and nature is a hallmark of who she is. If I was to write a novel and wanted a protagonist – one rich in character and earthy of spirit – that would keep the reader transfixed, I could do no better than using the Kiri-like character.

I love my work of helping authors, and getting their writing into a published book, and my time with Kiri was as good as it gets. We had many hours of discussion, on anything and everything. "Who inspired you?" I once asked her. Without hesitation, she said, "My biological father, and he still does, even though he is long gone".

Her stories, packed with wisdom and humour, are captivating and enriching. There is much in these writings that could be called wisdom, but in humility, Kiri would not call it wisdom. She would say "It just is, and the reader will take from it what he or she will".

Direction is so much more important than
speed. Many are going nowhere fast.

The good thing about getting old is that you don't
lose all the ages that you have been.

She must have written several hundred poems and as we chatted, she would often recite one. I am sure she remembers every poem she has written as I heard her recite dozens, all from memory. Kiri did not write the stories or poetry for others. She wrote them because they bubbled out, and wanted to be said. Her poetry though, was usually directed at a cause or injustice, where succinctly, she outlined her thoughts. Often the poems are about her second love – nature. I believe that her close family is her first love.

This biography is back and forth, as Kiri told it. You will also see some of the quotations she loved or developed. Also, interspersed, are some of her favourite poems that she wrote.

A dewdrop

Shimmering in the sun
Quivering in the breeze
I sit content
on the drooping lip
of an unfurled leaf
Crystal clear
a dewdrop pure
I fall to earth
I am no more

Remember, it doesn't have to be perfect to be wonderful. People don't have to be perfect to be wonderful.

CONTENTS

Testimonials
iii

Acknowledgements
iv

Dedication
v

A note from the publisher
vi

Preamble
1

Te Horo
18

Ruatoria
32

Whakawhitira
56

Back to Te Horo
74

1951
82

My life Story – Part 2
92

My life story – Part 3
118

My life story – Part 4
134

Bits and Pieces
152

A functioning Maori society
156

Quinten
162

My thoughts on death
166

Poetry
168

PREAMBLE

On the 23rd of June, 1937, I, Kiri Atahwai Tangaere made my debut into this wicked, yet wonderful world. I was born in the lounge room of my parent's farm, "Ekoe Station", in Rangitukia, the northernmost part of the east coast of the North Island of New Zealand. The homestead was called "Otirahorea".

At the time of my birth my father was in Auckland and my mother was home alone. The home was isolated because one had to cross the Maraehara River to get to it. Not a good time to make my entry into this world, as the river was flooding and almost over the river banks. Luckily, in those days we had telephones. These were called 'party lines' where about ten families had access to the same line. When we had a conversation, other parties could listen in. We were allocated numbers with a letter at the end. You could have 69D, 69K, 69R, and so on.

My mother rang my Uncle Tui Tuhaka and he caught our draught horse, 'Lady', and on Lady's back, crossed the flooded river. Upon arriving, my uncle was there to assist Mum deliver me.

In those days, most Maori mothers delivered their babies at home with one or two relatives in attendance. Mothers usually squatted on their knees on the floor and held on to a stool or box, while they were in labour, as this made the birthing easier. Times have changed and so have the methods. When I was older, my uncle often told me that if he knew I was going to be so naughty, he would have choked me on the way out, but I know he loved me. He was special to me.

I hate it when I am singing a song and the artist gets it wrong.

As we lose the old ones we know
that we have no one to replace them
because fewer and fewer remember a world
that knows another way. The loss of an old
one means not only the passing of a person but
it means the passing of a possibility of knowing
another way. This breaking is so profound that
only our hearts can know it.

My Dad

Anyway, my dad told me I was named after the dear old lady that raised him. She was from Manutuke. I will always remember the stories he told me of her.

When I was seven months old, my mother Hiria was hospitalised with tuberculosis, which was running rife in the country in the early 40's and 50's. I was taken by my father, Hunaara, and given to my mother's eldest sister and her husband, who were to take care of me. My father was reluctant to give me to them but he had to work and knew that I would be well looked after.

As often as you can take a walk
through nature and find a place that
makes you want to linger, "feel", and time
seems to stand still, and the serenity and
peace will overwhelm you, it is a sanctuary
that will re-energise your soul and spirit.

And still after all this time,
the sun never says to the earth,
"You owe me". Look at what happens
with a love like that – it lights up
the entire sky.

Kiri was the founding member of the women's circle, "Mana Wahine" (Raising Woman's Self Esteem), in 2011.

The group supports themselves; such as the time when one lady member returned home from a funeral to find her husband had stripped the house of furniture and everything of value, whilst he ran off with another lady. It did not take long for the group to restock the house with furniture. It is a safe place where all can tell of their troubles without sanction and in complete privacy.

Five of the first members

Memoirs of my life   7

Challenges are what makes life
interesting. Overcoming challenges is
what makes life worthwhile.

When my mother was released from hospital a year later, she and Pop came for me, but by this time, my aunt and uncle were the only parents I knew. They both cried. Pop didn't have the heart to take me from them, so I stayed. I was so privileged to grow up with Henry and Riwia Fox. They had no children of their own but over the years they raised eighteen of us. We were all told who our birth parents were so I always knew of my biological parents. I went to my biological parents for holidays but never really lasted the whole holiday. I got homesick and would ask to be taken home, but when my birth mother shouted at me, I definitely wanted to go back home. So Pop would drive me back to Te Horo. My biological parents had eleven children together – four females and seven males. Most Maori babies born during the war years were named after place names, events and countries that our Maori Battalion had fought at, as if a diary of events.

Pop and my Mother

I think that if I have learned
anything about friendship; it is to
hang in there, stay connected, fight for them
and let them fight for you. Don't walk away,
don't be distracted, don't be too busy or
too tired, and don't take them for
granted. Friends are part of the glue
that holds life and faith together
– powerful stuff.

Kiri formed Australia's Counsel of 13 Grandmothers. The purpose of the 13 Grandmothers is to represent and embrace the diversity of cultures in Australia, willingly sharing knowledge and wisdom with all, by telling stories of their life. Events are hosted all over Australia.

Counsel of 13 Grandmothers

The Pocketbook of Wisdom

Grandmother Kiri Dewes is a Maori Elder, poet and a very wise woman in her 80 somethings...

This book is a tribute to the much needed wisdom that Kiri has shared with so many around the planet.

Her sense of humour, kindness and compassion is renowned world-wide.

WIT AND WISDOM
FOR EVERY DAY

POCKETBOOK OF WISDOM

By Grandmother
Kiri Dewes
Australia's Counsel of
13 Grandmothers

13 Grandmothers book

We are all visitors to this time,
this place. We're just passing through.
Our purpose here is to observe, to learn,
to grow, to love, and then we return home.

When we sit and close our eyes another
world opens up and calms our minds,
so be still and hear, and know, be still
and see, be still and feel.

Inside everyone is a still small voice. Sometimes it is
necessary to close the eyes, to shut down our perceptions
to see.

Occasionally, when you are talking to people or children,
close your eyes and listen to them, listen to the tone of their
voices, listen to their excitement, to their pain, listen.

Today let us listen to what really counts.

The eldest in my biological family was my sister Heni-te-wa-moana but we called her Cissy. She was born while my mother's three brothers were at sea, on their way home from the war. So that is what her name means - Jane born while at sea. She married Joela Ryland of Tokomaru Bay. Together, they had their own family of ten, and took in anyone else who needed a mother and father. My sister was as poor as a church mouse, but always had a meal and a bed for anyone who was in need. She died aged sixty-nine, and was mourned by hundreds.

After Cissy, Nga-Hiwi-o-Kahimia was born, a male. He was such a gentleman, with never a harsh word for anyone. His name means "The Hills of Cashmere". My Aunty Paul named him in memory of her sweetheart who died of TB in a sanatorium on the hills of Cashmere in Christchurch on the South Island. We called him Hiwi for short. He was a school teacher all his working life. He married Bessie Tamati of Whareponga. They had five children of their own and adopted a daughter named Tracey. Next in line was Lou Hunaara. He was named after our Dad. We called him Louti. He married Elizabeth Dewes of Hicks Bay and they had four children.

Akuhata was next. He was named after our maternal grandfather. We called him Black. Black married Ruth Somerville of Foxton. They had three children. Both were in the teaching profession – in fact their entire family had been teachers.

Next was Katete Wehipeihana. We called him Cass. He was named after our family nurse. He married June Tamou of Wanganui, had their daughter, Whetu Aroha, and adopted their son Julian. Both Cass and June were also in the teaching profession.

After Cass came Tipuna-Taongakore-Mahue-Pani, who was named after a poor elderly relative who was orphaned at birth. We called him Nunu. Nunu married Zena Rangihuna of Tikitiki and they had eight children.

I was next, Kiri Atawhai. I married George Tamahori Dewes of Hicks Bay, and together we had seven children – three sons and four daughters. I lost two of my babies. A son aged three months, then a daughter who was stillborn.

After me, there was Tapita, a girl, and she was adopted by Wi Kaa and his wife. She died when she was eight years old.

Next was Taina Hoia, named after our Uncle Tom, who was overseas with the Maori Battalion. He was our mother's second youngest brother. Her name means younger soldier brother. She married Neil McGregor of Levin and they had five children.

Then there was Furlough, who died when he was still a baby. He was born when my uncles were on furlough.

The youngest was my baby brother, Patrick Rickard. Apparently, his name was longer, having been named after the biggest drunkards in Tikitiki, but he only used Patrick Rickard. He had two children. A son who was adopted by Cass and June and a daughter, Tania, who now lives in Townsville, Australia.

Between Mum and Pop and my biological parents I had fifteen brothers and sisters!

I love them all unconditionally and I am proud of who I am and proud also of my ancestry that descends through both my biological parents. My birth father I adored. He was such an inspiration to me. I was always over the moon just to be in his presence. I know it is because of him that I am so in love with my Maori heritage today. Even in death, he is my inspiration.

Loneliness

Loneliness is a feeling
that cannot be described
It is an emotion
an aching deep inside
Only you can feel it
only you know why
Sometimes it's so unbearable
you feel you want to die
The only thing that keeps you going
is knowing that one day
The reason for your loneliness
will soon be back to stay
The emptiness, the loneliness
will surely disappear
And you'll be reunited
with the one you hold so dear.

I wrote this poem for a wealthy lady whose partner was in prison for drugs.

> Kiri's birth mother was awarded the British Empire Medal for her services in the New Zealand Army.

At a global conference

Silence is golden unless you have children, then silence is suspicious.

Every closure is creating the way for a new beginning – an amazing beginning.

TE HORO

In my adopted family of eighteen, I was not familiar with them all because some had grown up and left home to make their own way in life. When I look back, I know without a doubt how lucky I was that they wanted to keep me. I believe that everything that happens to us on our earth walk is meant to be, and is all part of our journey. We all called our dad Pop and our mum was Mum (and even though she was in fact my Aunt, I happily called her Mum). They treated us all the same and we never wanted for anything.

Mum was a great gardener, growing flowers and vegetables. Her favourite flowers were standard roses, freesias, violets, daphne and gladioli. Our flower and our vegetable gardens were her pride and joy. I don't know how she kept up with everything. She was always making jam, preserving fruit, making pickles and relishes and preserving eggs. Meat and seafood were preserved by dropping them in fat. When she wasn't doing this she was in the garden weeding, getting vegetables for our meals or cooking and sewing for us all. Our larder was always full of preserves, pickles, jams and chutneys.

All the world's ugliness can be forgotten in an instant in the beauty of nature.

Finding your tribe. We all have the desire to find our tribe. A community of those that we feel comfortable with and nurture our journey. We need to establish a unique persona and have an intense desire for acceptance. Our tribe members are those who accept us as we are without reservation and gladly accompany us on our journey of evolution. With them we feel free to be our imperfect selves, to engage freely in activities we enjoy and express our vulnerabilities by relying on our tribe for support. Their reassurance helps us in our development.

Mum was also active in the community, doing her bit for the schools we attended. She was also a member and traveling delegate for the Tairawhiti Women's Welfare League, which took her away from home sometimes. I dreaded those times. I knew it was a break for her but home wasn't the same without her.

Once a month the Welfare League used to meet and they had competitions. Mum had entries in every competition, and did very well, collecting first prizes with her jams, sewing, needlework and crochet. Her crocheted work was displayed in many exhibitions. I entered some of my sewing and plants in the junior section and was always proud when I won prizes. In her early days, she was a school teacher in Hukarere Girls College in Hawkes Bay, along with my birth mother. They both taught there.

The Rose

You appeared a tiny node
Upon your mother's arm
Swelling gently swelling
Safe within your husky haven
Slowly creeping peering through
Are your tender petals
In close embrace
Sweetly caressing
Gracefully unfolding
In the warm rays of the sun
Pretty pink is your garment
With borders blushing red
You are strong
You're in full bloom
Your fragrance fills the air
You are, oh, so beautiful
Welcome to this world

I believe I witnessed the birth, the development and blossoming of a rose. In 2015, this poem took me to a Symposium in Washington, USA.

Mum also spun wool from the fleeces of our sheep, especially the black fleece. I used to sit at her feet and pull the wool while she sat at her spinning wheel peddling and rolling the wool through her fingers to form a fairly thick thread and, as it passed, it was wound onto a large bobbin. When there was enough on the bobbin, Mum would replace this one with another bobbin and keep spinning. I would then roll the wool off the full bobbin into a ball and place it in a basket. This was the procedure until we had spun enough for Mum to work with. She knitted all our cardigans and jumpers.

My sister Sue could spin wool too and she helped Mum knit for the family. I remember Mum knitted me fair-isle cardigans, jumpers, pixie hoods, berets, scarves and balaclavas. They aren't seen too often these days. Today it is far easier to buy these items as a lot of mothers work and they don't have the time to sit and knit. Mum taught me how to knit, crochet, use a sewing machine and do needlework.

Your influence is stronger than you know. Your decisions will show up in your children, and in your community.
The next generation is watching you,
and so let us show them how it is done.

Go out all day looking fabulous and I see no one I know. Go out for five minutes looking like crap and all of a sudden it's a damn reunion.

I love my excursions into the natural gardens, where the voice of the Great Creator is heard in the twittering of birds, the rippling of mighty waters, and the delightful, sweet breathing of flowers.

Mum insisted that I learn even though I was not interested. Now when I look back I realise how essential these skills were. How fortunate I was that she had the patience to teach me. I was more interested in going outdoors to play or go eeling in the creek or riding the horse, but now I am so grateful that I learnt so much from her because of her insistence.

> Kiri was born with a caul that covered her entire face (a caul is a net-like membrane that dries off and dissipates in time.) The stories go that sailors carry one for good luck and protection. They would purchase them for a lot of money.

As long as you keep waking up in the morning,
it is evident that the Creator is not through with
you.

Pop had a stroke and was paralysed down his right side. He could still talk but lost the use of his right hand and leg. His left leg was amputated just below the knee, and so he wore an artificial leg fitted in a boot. His socks were also specially made and from the age of ten it was my job to dress and undress him every day. I didn't mind this at all because I loved him dearly. He was my protector and always had the time to listen to whatever I had to say.

We lived out of town and every day he would ring for cigarettes and two bobs worth of McIntosh's toffees for me. I always made sure he remembered and would say, "Pop, don't forget my lollies." He was my hero. Whenever he needed me, he would whistle and I would know because it was a special whistle. He could still walk with the aid of a walking stick. When I was being naughty, Mum would try to catch me. I would run as fast as I could and sit or squat between his knees and he would keep her at bay with his walking stick.

Once you have heard the songbirds, known the swish of the long grass, and smelt the freshly tilled soil, you will never be happy about the city and towns that people carry, like a crippling weight upon their back.

Be grateful and celebrate the beauty in all things,
because beauty *is* everywhere.

He'd want to know what I had done to deserve a spanking and then decide whether it was worth a hiding. He always would stick up for me whether I was right or wrong. Mind you, I was a mischievous child and deserved a dressing down now and then.

Pop passed away in 1952, when I was fifteen years old. He was in his sixties. So I would say that my Pop had a good innings. For a long time after his death, I could still hear his whistle and it took me some time to accept that he was gone for always. Life goes on and we learn to accept, adjust and move on. So now, we only had Mum, and she was the backbone of our family. She was so strong for us all.

By this time, a lot of the family had drifted off to find work in the cities. Mum told me my baby years were spent in Te Horo close to my maternal grandparents. I don't really remember my grandmother. She died when I was two years old but my grandfather died when I was sixteen, so I got to know him quite well. He was a handsome old gentleman.

The Wrath of the Fires

Our love goes out to those
who perished in the fires
Our hearts are filled with sadness
for this tragic act of Nature
That has left families
friends and people worldwide
shocked and grieving
This is the prayer within our hearts
that those departed are safe
in the shelter of our Creators' arms
And those of us that remain
shall always be remembered
never to be forgotten.

Our hearts go out to the offspring of Tane
That suffered from the impact of the fires
No more do we hear the songs
nor the twittering of the birds
the vibrating trill of the cicada
the sounds of the animals
and those that creep and crawl
in the Great forest of Tane
The trees stand tall and naked
like statues in the desert
The hills and plains are bare
devastated by the fires.
Which were gifts from
the fingernails of Mahuika
But so abused by man...

The bushfires in 2009 inspired this poem. 135 people died in this conflagration, not to forget the creatures, in the Dandenong Ranges. The fires were not that far from my own home. There was ash on our windows and smoke filled the garden.

I believe in a world of people that respect and accept each other, the animals, and the beautiful nature that surrounds us. A world that is awakening to the memory of being one with all that is by gathering as many people as possible to be at peace in oneness. We together can raise to the vibration for the benefit of all.

RUATORIA

When I was three years old we moved from Te Horo to Ruatoria because Pop was the manager of the Ngati Porou Dairy Factory. The Ngati Porou Dairy Factory served the whole of the Tairawhiti district and the rest of New Zealand with butter and cream. It also provided work for the local people. Most of the people of the East Coast were dairy farmers and mixed farmers who ran cattle, sheep and pig farms.

I remember falling into our well at the back of our home one morning, in my nightdress. Lucky for me, my Nanny Kani came along and hooked me out with her walking stick. My friend, Puni Nepe, and I used to wander on down to the factory where the men would give us a handful of butter from the churn (butter straight from the churn tasted different). This was a daily treat for us.

We had beehives under our apple tree, and Mum used to warn Puni and me never to go there. However, one day when she was out shopping, on our way back from the factory, we thought we would sit on the beehives and enjoy our treats from the factory.

Let us appreciate the beauty of this earth
and celebrate each moment that we are out
in nature, for it constantly offers us simple
pleasures to love. Opening ourselves up to
the beauty around us is a way to bring more
happiness and peace in our lives.

Never be afraid to raise your voice for honesty,
truth and compassion against injustices, lying
and greed. If all the world's peoples did this, it
would change the world for the better.

Puni started swinging his feet and his boot constantly banged against the beehive he was on – that upset the bees. Out they came and attacked us both. We ran towards the house. By then, we were both covered in bees and screaming. My poor Pop came out as fast as he could and beat us with a towel with his one good hand.

Lucky for us, Mum returned from her shopping spree and removed the rest of the bees from us, then hurried us both into the bath. We were a sight for sore eyes. We could hardly open our eyes they were so swollen. Mum gave us no sympathy. Both our bodies were badly stung. She rang Puni's mum, who soon came over. She told us both that we deserved what we got, but we knew they did care. Mum put some kind of herb in our bath water to ease the pain and swelling.

Being a good person does not mean you have
to put up with other people's crap.

Those are two vivid memories I have of my days at the factory home we had. About half a mile from our home was a Gospel Hall and every Saturday we went there to watch movies. It cost sixpence each to get in, and a shilling for a large box of block toffee. The toffee kept us happy throughout the movie. We could buy gob stoppers too, and we did sometimes, but they were so big I could hardly fit one in my mouth. They cost a penny each. Everything was so cheap in those days compared to today's prices. We walked to the movies and walked home with my big brother Mac and my sister Monty.

When I was almost five we moved to Rotokautuku, a small farm that my grandma Kani gave my mum and Pop. My Nanny Kani and I used to go mushrooming together. After rain, our paddocks would have tons of mushrooms, and some were growing in circles so we called them fairy rings. I would run and sit in the middle of each one and make a wish. When I think about it, not one of my wishes ever came true.

Live for the beauty of your own reality. For me,
it's about being comfortable in my own skin.

Sometimes Nanny Kani would send Monty and Betty into the paddocks to dig for worms under the cow poop, for bait for Mum to go eeling. Of course, I tagged along too and when we couldn't be seen from the house, my sisters made me carry the spade. I would swing it and let it go and it would stick in the ground just ahead.

My sisters were walking in front of me and a little to the left. Monty was closest to me. Well, one of my shots at swinging the spade caught Monty's little toe and cut it off. She screamed and sat down as the blood flowed. My sister Betty bent down and saw the toe. I knew I was in trouble so I ran as fast as my bandy legs could carry me back to the house with Betty hot on my heels.

I was crying loudly so Mum would hear me. When Betty saw Mum she forgot about me and told Mum what happened to Monty. Mum told Betty off and said they were to blame because they should have carried the spade instead of giving it to me. I was off the hook.

Be a symbol of inspiration and make an impact
on others by following and chasing your
dreams and fulfilling them.

I always try to cheer myself up by singing.
Turns out, my voice is worse than my problems.

Memories

The sea is calm beyond the reef
And I am all alone
In the rocky sheltered haven
Of Port Awanui
My stamping ground in days gone by
Where once I roamed so free
The endless sky, the fresh sea breeze
The sand, the surf, and me
I close my eyes and all I see
Is how it used to be
The humble shacks upon the rise
The village down below
The women at their daily chores
The menfolk out at sea
The children playing happily

Down on the sandy shore
There's a deathly quiet now
Their laughter is no more
Just the cry of gulls, the crash of waves
Running to the shore
Time has changed so many things
There's not much left to see
Just the cry of gulls,
The crash of waves
Running to the shore
I still have my memories
Of what there used to be
In this place, this paradise
That's home sweet home to me.

I wrote this after a visit to the place where I grew up.

Pop had bought a Pontiac car in the forties. We were one of the few families who owned a car in those days. Anyway, Mac and Mum rushed Monty and her toe to the Te Puia Hospital where they were able to reattach it. I was never asked to carry the spade again.

Later, there were five of us children living with Mum and Pop. There was Mac, Monty, Tommy, Tony and I. Sue and Betty, my older sisters had left home. Sue had gone to Wellington to work and Betty had moved on to Rotorua.

I started school whilst living here. It was a three mile walk from our house at the top of the hill, to the Tapuwaeroa Junction, where we had to catch a bus to Manutahi Primary school in Ruatoria. This was a further six miles. Mac and Monty were the eldest at this time, then there was Tony, Tommy and I. Mum would tell Mac and Monty to give us a piggy back if we got tired. Mum bought each of us a pair of boots because there were only gravel roads in those days.

Memoirs of my life

Have a love affair with the wonder and beauty
of the earth. Cherish the sunset and each
sunrise, the wild creatures, and the wild places,
as they are truly your doorway to oneness.

We walked to the edge of the hill each morning and Mac would break a couple of branches off a cabbage tree. Tommy would break his own. Mac and Monty would sit on one each, and Tony and I would hang on behind them and we would slide down the hill. Then we would walk along the road from the bottom of the hill to the junction. Sometimes we would get a lift with someone but most days we would walk the distance. Often we missed the bus and so we walked all the way to school but always had fun on the way. The teachers used to praise us for walking the distance, even if we arrived at school at ten in the morning. If only they knew. A lot of times we missed the bus because we called in to Frank Bruce's orchard when the fruit was ripe or stopped at the creek to catch cockabullies (small fresh water fish).

Kiri, 20 years ago

We knew we missed the bus so we went on our way and stopped at the Waiapu River for a swim, and afterwards we would dry ourselves off by sitting on a rock in the sun. Mac always made sure we were neat and tidy when we arrived at school. The principal used to stand us up in front of assembly and praise our efforts for walking to school those nine miles.

There is a truth that I have learnt from life, and that is that some of the darkest times can bring us to the brightest of places. I have learnt that most toxic people can teach us the most important lessons, that our most painful struggles can grant us the most necessary growth, and that the most heartbreaking losses of friends can make room for new wonderful people. I have learnt that what seemed to be like a curse in the moment can actually be a blessing in disguise, and that what seemed like the end of the world is actually just the discovery that we are meant to travel down a different path. I have learnt that no matter how difficult things seem, we can't give up. We have to keep going. Even when it is scary, even when all our strength seems gone. We have to keep picking ourselves up and keep moving forward because whatever we are fighting with in the moment will pass and we will successfully make it through.

I remember once on my way to school, I was stung by a bumble bee, and by the time I got to school my left thigh was swollen and hard. I was taken to the staff room and treated by the nurse. Later, the Principal stood me up in front of assembly and told the children how brave I was. He lifted up my skirt and showed them the sting. I was so embarrassed because I had to pull down my knickers so they could see the swelling above my knee to my groin. Anyway, he praised my efforts for coming to school despite the bee sting. I seemed to be in trouble quite a bit with bees.

We always caught the bus from school each afternoon as far as the Tapuwaeroa junction, and walked the three miles from there to our home. We called into some orchards on our way, and sometimes we paddled in a creek before we climbed the hill. At a spot near the top of the hill, we always stopped at a spring adjacent to the road. Mac would clear the top of the water of any leaves, then he would lift us up, one at a time, to take a drink. The water was cold and welcome. This spring was called "Te mimi o Maraea" (Maraea's urine). That was in the forties and it is still there today.

Love is the most healing force in the world.
Nothing goes deeper than love. It heals not only
the body, not only the mind,
but the whole soul.

The things we do for ourselves are gone when
we're gone. What we do for others will remain
forever as our legacy. As your life is a message
to the world, make it inspiring, full of wisdom,
courage and strength. Your legacy lives on after
you are gone. Not one of us will live forever but
we can create something that will.

Some keep Sunday for going to church. I keep it
for staying at home with the chorus of the birds
my choir, in the sky above my chapel.

Mum always had a drink, and something to eat, ready for us when we got home. We took off our school uniforms and put on our home clothes. Mac, Monty and Tommy then went to the milking shed. We had eighty-two jersey milking cows. Mac used to stand in the yard and call the cows and they would look up and start walking to the cowshed from the paddock. Back then that was normal to me but now I look back and think how clever those cows were. Every one of them had a name.

I used to love going along to the cowshed with my hammer and mug when I was little, about four. The big ones hated me going with them but I didn't care. They used to tell me to go home, but Pop would tell them to leave me alone.

When they baled up the cows, I would pick all the ticks off their backsides. When I had a mug full, I would sit on the concrete and squash them with my hammer. The others were too busy to watch me. Mac got so angry with me because I would leave a big patch of blood on the concrete, which was difficult for them to wash it off. I was never popular with him in the cowshed.

I would sneak into the separator room and dip my fingers into the cream can and sometimes Mac would catch me and send me home. Instead of going home, I would go outside to the pig's trough and paddle my hands and feet in the curdled milk. It stunk but that didn't matter to me. Some got on my clothes, and when I got back to the house, Mum would tell me I stunk, and order me into the bathtub. After school each day, I would go to the cowshed.

The Humpback Whale

Gracefully cruising, the giant humpback
Plunges deeply into the cold blue ocean
Crooning softly
As he joins the pod
Searching for sustenance on the ocean floor
Then rising swiftly to shatter the surface
For a welcome blast of air
A glimpse of blue sky
A kiss from the wind
And the humpback's gone again
Down into the blue
The deepest blue
In the sea of Tangaroa

My son Patrick asked me to write a poem about a whale.

Some Friday afternoons, I would spend the weekend with our neighbours, Whai, his wife Nursey, and their children. They lived about three miles further up our driveway. Her eldest daughter Rawinia was my friend. We all called her Lovey. They had a big farm and had natural gas on it. Their house had two rooms and the walls were made of corrugated iron. Around the top of the walls were perforated steel pipes, and each night they would throw a match up and the pipes would burst into flame. Not only was this the source of light but it also kept the house warm.

Whai was always away working. Nursey and her children were home on their own a lot and I loved going there. When I first went there in the mid-forties, there were only three children. There was Lovey, Bill and Emily. I was still visiting them when the next three were born. They were tough children. They walked over the hill to the Mangaoporo junction to catch the bus to Whakawhitira School. It was a far walk for them but they never complained. Some days were really cold, wet and windy but they never missed a day of school.

Nature inspires my everything. She inspires my solitude, my writing. She lifts me upon her welcoming wings and soars me through the sky of possibilities. She colours my day, brightens my soul and calms my nights. She is fierce and beautiful, strong and delicate, an unrelenting Queen. She is ever wary of new beginnings – in spring a colourful maiden; in winter a wise old lady; in autumn a looking glass to my falling-leaf-self; and summer a warmed, blossoming benefactor and woman to the sun.

My school days at Manutahi Primary were good ones but it all ended when my big brother Dudu came home from the war and brought his new wife home to Rotokautuku. Dudu was in the air force during the war, and when he returned, he met and married Dorothy Fergusson of Wairoa. At that time, we were still milking eighty-two cows and had quite a few pigs and horses.

My favourite animal was Midnight, a black horse. He had a patch on the left side of his stomach that looked like a gumboot. He was tame and little children could ride him. Anyway, Mum left Rotokautuku farm to Dudu and Dot, and we moved not too far away. I missed the farm, especially going to the cowshed with my mug and hammer to squash the cow ticks, sloshing in the pig trough, riding the horses, and picking mushrooms with my Nanny Kani.

Please can I borrow a hug – I promise I will give
it back to you with interest.

Whoever enters your life is the right one. No
one comes into our lives by chance.
Everyone who is around us, anyone with
whom we interact with represents something,
whether to teach us something or to help us
improve a current situation.

Nanny Kani died while we were living here. I could still hear the shuffle of her slippers as she walked around the house. It felt really strange without her presence in our house. When I think about it, Mum must have missed her a lot because she was raised by her.

Where are you

Where are you, the leaders, the elders
to paddle the canoe of knowledge
Arise and come forth to teach our children
and young people who are yearning,
searching for the treasures of our ancestors
Our hearts cry out for their gifts
Alas, the yearning goes on.
The storytellers, fluent orators and songstresses of old
have journeyed on through the gateway
to the Spirit World
Our hearts cry out for the gifts of our ancestors.
Alas the yearning goes on.
Our youth are grasping what little they see and hear
It's time to pull together and teach our unique language
So our young, our descendants can stand
tall and proud In the days ahead
and into the future
Our hearts cry out for the gifts of our ancestors
Alas, the yearning goes on.

I wrote this as a message and plea to the Maori Elders
living here in Australia, to come together and teach our
young ones our language and culture,
so that it never dies.

WHAKAWHITIRA

We lived at the foot of the hill about a mile from the Mangaoporo Junction. I liked our home there. We had many fruit trees and beautiful flower gardens. It wasn't too long before Mum was organising our vegetable gardens. We had paddocks planted with potatoes, kumara, pumpkin, kamokamo (marrow) and watermelon. Our potatoes and kumara were planted so they would last from season to season. Harvesting our crops was a family task and we took time off school to help.

By the time we moved to Whakawhitira, my sister Monty had gone to a school in Featherston and Mac was working in Ruatoria. He used to ride our draught horse Nugget across the Waiapu River every day to work. Nugget was one of our most valuable assets because, not only did he take Mac to work, he pulled the plough that ploughed and tilled the soil in the paddocks ready for planting. He also pulled the sledge and cart that carried our wood for the winter.

Tommy, Tony and I had to go to Whakawhitira School as it was closer for us. We walked half a mile each day to catch the school bus at the Mangaoporo junction. From there it took fifteen minutes to our school. I enjoyed my time at this school.

Although life isn't always fair, it is still wonderful.

Be only with cheerful friends. The grouches pull you down.

One day on our way to school there were four of us sitting on the back seats of the school bus and two of my mates 'let off'. The smell, so bad, drifted up to the front of the bus. The driver pulled over to the side of the road, stood up and asked, "Who farted?" No one owned up so he ordered all four of us to get off the bus, and we had to walk to school. We were not allowed back on the bus for one week. Mum was mad with me when I told her. However, I was allowed to ride Nugget to school for that week. I was happy because each morning I picked up my mates along the way, and we all four rode Nugget. It was fun.

Whenever the bus passed us, we would wave to the bus driver. He pretended he didn't see us, but we knew he could. I mean, who could not see four kids riding a draught horse along the side of the road on the bus route?

I had some cousins at this school. They were the Collier family. Their paternal grandmother was a sister to my maternal grandfather and I felt good knowing this as we didn't know anyone else when we first went to this school. The school had three classrooms. Every morning when the bell rang we would have assembly. First, we would say, "Good morning" to the three teachers, sing a hymn, then it was time for 'toothbrush drill' and 'fingernail inspection'

Each child had their own small jar. Two children were chosen to fill the jars with salt and water and that is what we brushed our teeth with. The teachers would walk along the rows and inspect our nails. This was a daily event before we entered our classrooms.

We studied Morse code at this school, and it was great. It came in handy for recognising phone calls and sending messages to each other from the classroom to the school house. Our principal at this time was Mr Prosser. His wife was the infant mistress and they had a son called Anthony. They came from England and I have fond memories of them. I sometimes spent weekends with them. I met my first true friends at this school. They were Hinerau, Babbington and Edna Nukunuku. We all called Hinerau 'Pussy'. We did a lot together, like horse riding, swimming in the river and biking.

Our mothers were great friends. Edna was a real tough girl at school. If she thought someone was being mean to me she would tell them off or threaten to beat them up. In fact, all her brothers and sisters were strong and no one wanted to be their enemy. These two special friends are still dear to me. I live in Melbourne, Australia and whenever I went home to New Zealand, I always made the effort to ring Edna who lived in Wainuiomata or meet up with her just to catch up and keep the threads of friendship going. Although I love Australia, NZ is my home, my spiritual home.

Te Horo

Te Horo is my special place, my home sweet home
Nurtured by my elders and kindred folk
The-Calling-Hills-of-Rakaitemania
The sentinel, the shelter of my people,
Ngati Horowai, subtribe of my people
Rakaitemania and Iwirakau
My ancestors Chief and Chieftainess of this Marae
Tawaroa is the resting place of my elders
And my many much loved relatives
I sit in front of my ancestral house
And think of the ocean of tears
That flowed in the forecourt
For our loved ones who have journeyed
Down the pathway of the Goddess of Death
Rest in the sheltering arms of the creator
The fluent orators of the Marae are no more
The elders with the knowledge
Of ancient stories, traditions and songs

We, the descendants are striving,
Seeking, learning, holding on
So that we may never lose the treasures
The teachings, weaving, carving, chants
Genealogy, proverbial sayings
And so much more
To pass on to future generations
so that they will never be lost
To always return to the trails of their ancestors
Infusing and strengthening them spiritually
So they will stand tall and proud in this troubled
And ever changing world
The place where I grew up.
That's home sweet home to me.

The girls wore green rompers and white blouses. The boys wore black shorts and green shirts. The girls were never happy to wear rompers. They looked like bloomers with pleats in front. I guess we were at the age where we were starting to care about how we looked to the opposite sex. During the war years, I regularly accompanied my mother to the local Marae in Whakawhitira.

They had fundraisers for the Maori Battalion. Some nights there would be 'Flag five hundred'. Other nights there would be 'Euchre'. Mum would tell Mac to get Nugget harnessed to the cart, ready for us to go to the Marae. Mum was a good driver. She would always make sure we were warm for our half-hour cart trip to Tinatoka Marae.

I looked forward to these evenings at the Marae because Pussy would be there. While the adults played cards, we played outside with the other kids from our school. When the card games ended, we would all have supper together before we went home. There were prizes for the winners of each session. First prize was usually a bag of flour or a bag of sugar – these were precious in those days. Second prize was a large camp-oven bread, crockery of some sort, and third prize was butter and jam dishes, milk and sugar sets, or drinking sets. I thought that the prizes were great.

When I look back on those times, I know that our women were strong, hard-working, women. Not only in

How to make a house a home? Your home is your refuge. So fill it up with what you love, surround yourself with family and friends, music, plants and hobbies.

The strength of a woman is not measured by the impact that her hardships in life have had on her – but is measured by the extent of her refusal to allow these hardships to dictate to her and who she becomes.

their homes but in the community. There was great community spirit, especially while many of our men were away at war, so a lot of the men's work fell on the shoulders of the women and their families.

As a girl growing up I took so much for granted because all my needs were met. I never wanted for anything – my mother made sure of that – so I never knew or really understood why so many people were in need. I remember Mum packing food and clothing into parcel lots and putting them into a large sack that was slit down the middle, where it straddled Nugget's rump. We called these sacks 'pikau bags'. Every Maori family that owned horses had pikau bags. They were handy for carrying things in. Anyway, I would sit behind Mum on Nugget as she delivered the food and clothes packages to people she knew needed help. She was such an amazing person.

I'm not sure if washing machines were invented in the early forties, but I know we never had one. The only appliances Mum had to help her with the washing was her scrubbing board and a four gallon kerosene tin to boil water in. Yes, they certainly were tough women in the forties; we never heard them complain. Saturday was laundry day for us and Nugget would be prepared to haul us and our dirty washing down to the Mangaoporo River.

Find a voice and speak your truth. Each of us is an original. Each of us has a distinctive voice. When you find it, your story will be told and you will be heard.

We picked up our neighbour, Tangitangi Takurua, her four children and my two brothers, Tommy and Tony. They came along because Mum and Tangitangi always packed a lot of food and goodies for us to eat and they didn't want us to miss out. Mum and Tangitangi put up a clothesline on the river bank and as they finished a tubful, they would peg them on the line to dry. By the early evening our washing was hung, dried, folded and put back in the baskets. Mind you, we'd be munching on food throughout the day and by this time we were ready to go home. Our cart was loaded with our clean washing and other gear we took with us. Nugget would tow us all back to our homes.

Television wasn't around then but we had a radio, a very old Philips brand, and Mum always listened to the Maori News at 9.00 pm. Electricity wasn't in our area back then, so Mum had two batteries to run the radio. One was always in Ruatoria getting charged so that when one lot was flat the other was ready to use, so we were able to use our radio all the time. Mum and Pop had their regular serials that they listened to. These were the only times Mum sat still in daylight hours.

Other than that, she was always pottering around the house or the garden. Mum bought us comics, such as: Captain Marvel, The Phantom, Ginger Meggs, and a few others that were popular in those days. She also bought us a few jigsaw puzzles. These kept us happy in the evenings or on rainy days. I can't remember ever being bored.

Memoirs of my life 67

Kiri at an event in Colac supporting indigenous land rights in the Pilbara Mountains

I loved the creek behind our home. There were quite a few willow trees growing along the banks, and the pink roots were visible in the water. I often went eeling in the creek. I'd feel with my hands under the banks and in the willow roots until I located eel holes. There would be two holes, not too far apart, and I would feel between the holes and feel an eel. I'd curl my fingers around the body of the eel and pull it out slowly and throw it up on the bank, then hit with a heavy stick. I was good at this. I was like Mum, where I loved eeling, but never ate them. I walked up and down the creek; I reckon I knew every eel hole along the way. Mum used to give the eels and whitebait that we caught to people who loved them. That was nice. At least there was always someone to give them to.

I'm sure I was meant to be a boy because I did jobs that were really boy's jobs. I liked chopping wood for our fires. Tommy and I had to climb the hill behind our house to get spring water for us to drink, as we were dependent on tank water. We carried a four gallon drum of water each from the spring. It wasn't too bad as it was a downhill trip.

Our house never had a bathroom or laundry. Our stove was an 'Orion' stove model that was around in the thirties and forties. A water tank was built into the side of it and it was my job to make sure it was always full. We washed our dishes with this water, and Mum used it to wash us.

We had a cast iron oval tub that we washed ourselves in, watched by Mum's eagle eyes, to make sure we got the green grass stains off our knees. I can remember her scrubbing our heels with an eaten corn cob.

Because of the limited hot water, Tommy and Tony were always washed first. I was last so I had to empty the tub of water over the creek bank in the dark. I was scared of the dark. At night it was spooky outside our house because there was a pine hedge around the house. Beyond the garage were tall pines that swayed and creaked on windy nights.

Sentinel of Waikanae

Lonely tree laying there
On the beach at Waikanae
A sorry sight to see
You have no clothes
Your arms are gone
Your body is left laying here
Your skin has peeled
Your head is bald
Your fingers are all broken
What a melancholy end
Once you grew, stood tall
And proud In the Great forest of Tane
A shelter for his children
In time you fell
Swept into the river
By the tears of the Sky Father
Carried out to sea
Flung ashore
By the waves of Tangaroa
And here you lie
Your head thrust seaward
Sentinel of Waikanae.

I drove Nugget when he pulled our plough to till the soil in our paddocks ready for planting. I loved sitting on the sledge with the cream cans. Mac steered Nugget, who was towing the sledge to the cream stand down on the road side, ready for the driver of the cream truck to pick up and take to the dairy factory in Ruatoria. I liked sliding down the hill on cabbage tree leaves, bits of tin or bits of carpet. These were fun things to do as children. We played hopscotch and were always in trouble because we would scrape the floor polish out of the tin before it was empty and use it to play. Mum wasn't pleased at all.

We were still living in Whakawhitira when I attended Pae-o-te-riri High School in Tikitiki. This was about seven miles north-east of Whakawhitira. As usual, I caught the bus from the Mangaoporo junction and the other students from my class in Whakawhitira all came to the high school on the same bus. It was a big move for us as our new high school was bigger than our old school. It was good because we all knew each other. We kept together for a while until we got to know our new classmates. Of course, we were all in the same classroom and that was good. I spent one year at this school and I enjoyed my year there. I saw quite a lot of my biological siblings because my sister Taina lived with our Aunty Paul, whose house was next to our playground. Taina moved to live with her because it was closer to school. I spent some weekends with them so that we could go to the movies together.

Be unpredictable, be random, and just go, just do. Keep growing, learning, changing. You are never the same person, and there's one thing you can be aware about yourself – do what you want to do and be who you want to be.

Our church at Tikitiki

Yes, there was a cinema theatre in Tikitiki but we called it a picture hall in those days. Mena Kururangi was the guy who ran the movies every Saturday night. He was quite a funny man. Of course, by this time in my life, a few of my friends and I had boyfriends. When the lights were switched off, ready for the movie to begin, the boys climbed over the seats and sat with us. Mena would switch the lights on and off and the boys would duck down so Mena couldn't see them. It was quite funny. We'd look back and Mena would be laughing at us.

After the movies the boys would walk my sister and I home. It was great because they really did look after us. I guess it was a new experience having a boyfriend. I didn't think any guy was attracted to me because I was such a tomboy. I was always wearing my brother's shirts, pants and knee high stockings, happily I was wrong.

Be fearless in the pursuit of what sets your soul on fire.

BACK TO TE HORO

I was thirteen by now and started paying more attention to myself. I took care of my hair and wore dresses and skirts more. My big sister Sue came home from Wellington with her baby boy. Mum kept the boy and sent Sue back to Wellington to work. He was like a brother to me. We called him Buddy.

Meanwhile, a brand new home was being built for us back in Te Horo to live in. Mum had sent Tony to St. Stephens College in Auckland and Tommy had moved to Wellington to work. I know Mum was happy to go home to Te Horo. We took Nugget with us but he kept getting out of the paddock and going back to Rotokautuku, so Mum told Dudu to keep him there.

Our new house was lovely. It had three bedrooms, and for the first time in my life I had a bedroom of my own. My most vivid memories start here in Te Horo. Our house was built next door to my maternal grandparents' home, and situated on the lower slopes of the hills opposite our Marae.

The hills were known to our people as 'Nga-Puke-Karangaranga-a-Rakaitemania', which means 'The calling hills of Rakaitemania'. Te Horo is a peaceful little settlement nestled between rolling hills that rise up from the lowlands of the Waiapu Valley.

Learn that rules can be broken. Be bold enough to live life on your terms and never ever apologise for it.

It is here that my mother's people come from. The Waiapu River wends its way from the foothills of our tribal mountain 'Hikurangi' – The Sky Piercer. In speech making our river, Waiapu and our mountain, Hikurangi are acknowledged. Te Horo is close to the mouth of the river. The first port along the east coast was at Te Horo, and it was called Port Awanui. It still functioned when my parents were living but now only fragments of the wharf and village can be found.

The children of Te Horo all went to the beach there to play, swim and gather seafood with our uncles. We played while they dived for abalone, crayfish, sea eggs and mussels. Some of us collected crabs and cockles. When we returned home, whatever we got from the ocean was shared with the community.

Te Horo was also our Marae and our Chieftainess was Rakaitemania. Our meeting house bears her name. She was well before my time so what I know of her was learnt through studying our history and genealogy. Through her, I belong to 'Ngati Horowai,' a subtribe of Ngati Porou.

This is one of the many tribes of New Zealand and were the descendants of the canoes of 'The Great Migration' that crossed the Pacific Ocean from the islands of the Pacific to New Zealand in the year 1350 A.D. Every tribe and subtribe had a chief but in Ngati Porou some of our leaders were women, and so our meeting houses bore their names. In fact, Ngati Porou had many matriarchs and their stories are recorded in our history books. So Rakaitemania was our matriarch and leader.

In her day, a means of communication with her people was to climb the hills above our Marae and relay her messages vocally to the people, where someone would hear it and relay it along the Waiapu Valley. The people would know whether there was a wedding, funeral or gathering of some sort.

By now, I'm sure you know a little about my Te Horo. The place where I was deposited when I was seven months old and continued my journey from here to Ruatoria, Rotokautuku, Whakawhitira and back to Te Horo. From our house, we look down on our Marae. There is a gentle slope from our house to get there. The main road runs between our house and the Marae.

There were four tennis courts on the Marae, and my three uncles: Tom, Peter and John were great tennis players. I remember watching my Uncle Tom playing. He was awesome to watch. Every time he hit the ball, he'd give a little grunt and his ball would always find its mark. He was also a star on the football field. When his team played in Tikitiki, which was across the river from Te Horo we would cross the river on horseback just to see him play.

He was like a bullock as he ploughed through the opposition. I usually got to ride the family horse, called Donkey, to these games and we always made it across the Waiapu. Donkey knew the crossing with his eyes closed.

Eagles Rest

There's a peaceful little haven
That I love called 'Eagles Rest'
Where the views out to the ocean
Are among the very best
Hear the keening call of songbirds
Welcoming the breaking dawn
Telling every living creature
To awake for it is morn
Slowly Tama-nui-te-ra rises up beyond the hills
Adding all his warmth and blessings
To the symphony of trills
The little town of Foster
Nestles sweetly in the vale
Safely sheltered by the trees
From any storm and gale

This place is so inspiring, it's a poets paradise
Nature's beauty at its best
Nestled here 'neath southern skies
Up here in 'Eagles Rest'
Stands the homestead perched up high
Girthed with trees, shrubs and flowers
Set in simple symmetry
Wongan is the queen here, a real contented cat
A fussy little tabby, the boss, and she knows that
Junitta is her keeper and little did she know
Wongan would keep her busy and always on the go
They keep each other company
when they are on their own
In 'Eagles Rest' their paradise, their 'Home sweet home'

Our Marae consisted of the 'kautu', which is our cookhouse and dining room, a meeting house, our ancestral building, a church, a cemetery, toilets, and four tennis courts. There were four houses close to the Marae. When I returned to live in Te Horo, there were four families near the Marae.

Next to us lived Uncle Tom and Aunty Roki with my grandfather. The children with them were Tommy, Coby and Peanut. Across the road on one side of the Marae lived Harry Haenga and his wife Ripeka. They had no children of their own, but adopted Waiapu Pepere, Herewini Ngata, and for some time had Sue Cooper and Mickey Tamati. The other side of the Marae lived Dick George and his wife Hana. They raised a few children but I only knew Eru Paenga, Wharepa Tibble and Wally Milner. Eru was away in the army so I never got to know him until a lot later. In our house was Mum, Pop, Buddy and me. So living around the Marae were eleven children.

We all played on the tennis courts most afternoons after school but not before we had done our home duties, like cutting wood and kindling to start the fire in the morning. All the stoves were wood burners so we had to make sure that the wood box was always full for Mum. Buddy was too young, and Pop wasn't able do the chores.

We had a flash stove now, and a hot water cylinder cupboard next to it. There were shelves above the water cylinder, which was great for airing the washing and storage. No more carting or heating water as our new cylinder took care of that. Between our houses and Port Awanui lived three more families.

Hemara and Kiri Te Maro and their family of four. Nehe and Hohi Wawatai and their family were further along. Some of them had already left home and eight were still there. The last house before the Port belonged to George and Tawai Pepere and their family. Their sons, Davy and John, often rode on their horses to the Marae to play with us. Sometimes the Wawatai children would join us too. We played tennis, tiggy, squinch, and hide and seek. We'd play till dark then Mum would tell us all to go home.

Life always offers you a second chance. It's called tomorrow. Your life is what it is from the choices you made. If you do not like your life, it's time to make better choices.

1951

I was really settled in our new home and attending Manutahi Technical School in Ruatoria. This was eighteen miles from Te Horo. There were three of us from Te Horo who caught the bus at the junction at the foot of the hill each day to school. Ganny Wawatai, Teao Wawatai and I.

The other road at the junction went almost to the mouth of the Waiapu River to a settlement called Tikapa. The school bus went as far as Tikapa to pick up all the children from there. By the time it returned it was quite full. Luckily, half a mile from the junction was Waiomatatini Primary School and many of the children got off here.

Adults also used the bus to travel to Ruatoria to do their shopping as it was the nearest place to shop. From the mouth of the Waiapu River, on the side where we lived, the first settlement was Tikapa, then Te Horo, Waiomatatini, Kakariki, then over the Kainanga Hill to Ruatoria.

The township of Ruatoria had a picture theatre, billiard saloon, barber shop and post office, Hunter's Bookshop. Loan and Mercantile, Williams and Kettle, Thompson's Saddlers, Ned Kaiwai's second hand shop and taxi service. There was a butcher shop, service station, the Kiwi Tearooms, Charlie Connelly's Fish and Chip Shop, and the Manutahi Hotel. I guess no place is complete without a pub. There were two other taxis owners in Ruatoria: Charlie Connelly and Snowy Mathieson. Later, I drove a taxi in Wellington, but more on that later. So you see Ruatoria was quite a Boom Town in the early forties and fifties.

My high school days were happy ones at Manutahi Technical School. I played hockey and basketball for the A team. We often travelled to play against other high schools. I also played hockey for our home team – we were called Porourangi. The team was named after a founding ancestor from our area.

My cousin Polly Tuhaka and I were the left and right wingers in our team. I loved the sport and would do anything to please Mum so she would let me go to the weekend hockey matches. If I did anything to displease her, she would say "You're not going to play hockey today," but my dear old Uncle Tui, who was our coach, would come in the bus to Te Horo to pick me up. He would get out of the bus and call out to my mother and say, "Where's that girl?" and Mum would call back and say, "She's coming," and as I'd run through the door she'd glare at me and say, "Wait till you get home." By the time I got home she had calmed down. I often deserved a kick in the butt but I never got one.

Pop never agreed with physically hitting us as a punishment but he took away our privileges or grounded us. To be honest that never worked. He'd feel sorry and let us off every time. Sometimes when I went to play hockey in Ruatoria I wouldn't come home. Instead, my cousin Polly Tuhaka and I would hang around town so we could go to the dance at Mangahanea, a mile out of Ruatoria.

They had a dance evening there nearly every Saturday and the band was Jack Fish and His Boys. Jack was good on the saxophone. The dances then were: the 'Gay Gordon', 'The Twist', 'Rock'n'roll', the 'Scabby Dog Rag', 'Samba', 'Tango', 'Rhumba', 'Charleston' and of course, the 'Waltz' and 'Foxtrot'. Anyway, I would sneak an outfit for the dance into my hockey bag before I left the house. I would go home after the dance with my Uncle Tui and Polly, and they would drop me off.

Every time there was a dance in Ruatoria I would go and Uncle would tell Mum I was with him and she was okay with that. She never knew I was going to the dances till one night I came home after midnight and snuck into my bedroom and she was in my bed. She tried to stop me from playing hockey but my uncle Tui always made the bus driver come and pick me up. I wasn't interested in boyfriends I was too busy having a good time with my cousins and friends.

I was happy catching the bus or bumming a ride to town on 'Karuwai'. Karuwai was the name of George Pepere's truck. It was the only vehicle in Te Horo. Even Tikapa never had a vehicle. Every Saturday, anyone from Te Horo who wanted a ride into Ruatoria was picked up by George on Karuwai.

Earth and sky, forest and fields, lakes and rivers, seas and the mountains are excellent teachers. What they teach us can't be learnt from books.

Poor old Karuwai was always sagging on a Saturday taking us all to play hockey and football at Whakarua Park in town. Ruatoria had a park with a grandstand and the park was large. Most times, we'd all head home on the back of Karuwai and stop at the top of Kainanga Hill to let the crew off to relieve themselves. That hill was known by us as Mimi Hill. There's a little story about this hill. There was a lizard that had a nest there. It is said that someone stole it and a curse was put on the hill. It always slips and a lot of the hill has disappeared into the Waiapu River – it will always slip till the mother finds her baby. Many a time we couldn't get to school because of slips on Kainanga Hill. Sometimes we'd be at school and there would be a slip on Kainanga and we'd have to stay in town till the road was cleared. I always stayed with my Uncle Charlie Wilkie and his wife. They were very kind to me.

My Uncle Charlie owned all the buses in Ruatoria, and they all had Maori names; Iritekura, Ta Apirana, Atu and Uepohatu. His bus depot and home were on the edge of town heading out to Waiomatatini. They were the most flash buses in the Tairawhiti district, all painted red with black and white trimmings. The largest bus was 'Ta Apirana' This was the bus that took us to school each day. My Uncle Charlie took great care of his buses. They were always shining and clean. Our bus driver was Jim Keefe, and he was a good driver.

Our school was opened when I was a student there. I remember the Minister of Education was a Mr Algie. He came up from Wellington for the opening. It was a grand event. The day started with a traditional Maori welcome for the VIP's, followed by a performance by the school Maori Culture Club. Sadly, the majority of the Maori Elders who attended are no longer here.

I remember my English teacher Mr Dawes. Every time I went to his class, I'd go to sleep. In fact, a few of us did. There was something about his voice. Then there was our music class. No one wanted to stand next to Lovey Tako because she sang loud and flat. My favourite subjects were Maori and English. Clothing didn't interest me then, neither did Home-craft. I enjoyed woodwork, art and sports.

At the end of each year, we had a social at the school, which was held outdoors on our assembly courtyard. The courtyard was lit up with floodlights, and all the students, when dressed up, looked so grown up. By my last year in high school I guess most of the girls in our class had dated someone from school. Our socials were a lot of fun. There were novelty dances. I remember winning the Statue Waltz with Kapa Keelan. He was such a shy boy.

I was seventeen when I finished school and went to Victoria University to study Early Child Education. I was a good student, but more important to me was that everything that I learnt, I converted into Maori concepts. Later, I opened a Maori child care centre in Pomare. I ran this for six years. At University, the Director congratulated me for my Maori work and said I was a wonderful role model. Not bad considering some of the schools that I attended banned the use of Maori.

I ended up with a Bachelor of Arts degree in Social Science and Maori Studies. I also did a year of art at University and loved it.

Qualifications

At the time of putting the book together, Kiri was determined to not have reflected all of her various qualifications. So other than sharing her Bachelor of Arts degree in Social Science and Maori Studies with you, I can say that when going through her documents there were many certificates, citations, testimonies, and awards.

I started teaching at Waiomatatini School as a Junior Assistant. My brother Hiwi taught there before me. It was all new to me but the Principal and his wife were good to me. I enjoyed my year there. I stayed with Mum in Te

Horo still. Meanwhile, my sister Sue had married, and she and her husband Jim Porou, and their three boys, moved in with us. I loved my nephews dearly but I moved to Ruatoria into the Teachers bach with seven other female teachers. That was a new experience for me.

There were six of us staying together. I remember one night there were three of us in the bath and I happened to look up at the window, which was quite high and saw two faces looking down at us. These two guys, who we knew, had climbed the apple tree just outside the bathroom window. We got out of the bath quickly, wrapped towels around us and took off to catch the two culprits but they got away on their horses. By then we realised we were in the main street in our towels so we hurried back to the bach. From then on, we were very careful to draw the curtains whenever we took a bath.

I caught the bus each morning to Waiomatatini School for the rest of the year before moving back to Te Horo. I couldn't concentrate on my studies with so many of us in our house so I moved to Tikapa to stay with my Dad's sister, Aunty Bella, and her husband, Uncle Buster.

They had a big family. When I went to live with them, Billy, Fred, James and Mary were the only children still living at home. I loved my aunt, uncle and my cousins. They let me have their bach to stay in. It was away from the house, but near the main road, so I just walked out the front of the bach to catch the bus to work. It was so handy and I loved having a little pad of my own to live in. Mind you, I missed my Mum, so I made sure to visit her as often as I could.

I spent two years teaching at Waiomatatini School. Then I got a transfer to Hicks Bay Primary School. The hardest thing for me to do was to leave Mum. I remember when I went by the gate, I felt sick inside. I knew I was moving out of the area and wouldn't be able to see her as often as I would have liked.

At the end of the last term of school at Waiomatatini, my father was waiting for me at the school gates. He and I went back to Te Horo to pick up my clothes and other gear. I had made up my mind to go to work in the Post Office in Wellington, instead of going to Hicks Bay. My Dad had other plans. I did not want to be a school teacher. He told me I had to honour my agreement to go to Hicks Bay, and that was why he came to pick me up. After saying goodbye to Mum and Pop, my Dad and I took my belongings to my brother Hiwi and his wife Bessie's house. They were living in one of the Hicks Bay School houses right next door to the school.

Maori Community Music

Victoria Maori Festival Committee Inc. (and the NZ chapters). Kiri was a judge for twenty-nine years, and was invited to festivals all over. However, at seventy-seven she declined, as with her poor hearing, she felt she would not be fair to the contestants.

MY LIFE STORY – PART 2

After unloading my gear at Bessie and Hiwi's house, Pop told me he wanted me to go to Ngaruawahia with him. So after a cuppa with Hiwi and Bessie, Pop and I drove to Omaio, where we stayed the night with Pop Gage. Three of my father's friends were waiting for us. There was Horace Lewis, John Tibble, and Pop Gage. We travelled together to Ngaruawahia.

I found out on our way there that this day was a grand event. It was the opening of "Mahinarangi", a beautiful carved building on Turangawaewae Marae in Ngaruawahia, the centre of the King Movement. At that time, King Koroki was the Paramount King of the Tainui tribe. His mother was Princess Te Puia, who was still living then. She was responsible for the building of Mahinarangi. She went to Waiomatatini in the Tairawhiti District to ask Sir Apirana Ngata of the Ngati Porou tribe for carvers to help with the carving of Mahinarangi. He took his master carvers to assist with the work and completion of this unique building.

Anyway, we left Omaio early next morning, stopped in Te Teko for breakfast and arrived in Ngaruawahia about 10.00 am. As soon as we got out of the car, we were led to the King who was seated in front of the main stand. His ten bodyguards flanked him. It was an unusual sight for me to see. I tried to tell Pop that I'd wait in the car for him

Beauty

I sit engrossed in thoughts of beauty
A new born babe so pure, so chaste
The elegant flight of the snow white heron
The infinite wisdom of age
The echoing roar of rolling thunder
The warming rays of the sun
The welcome calm that follows the storm
The guiding light of the moon
The heavens pierced by the flash of lightning
A tree aflame with bloom
The view of a distant
snow-capped mountain
The waking glow of dawn
In all God's wondrous handiwork
There's beauty to behold.

but he wouldn't hear of it. He steered me along in front of him and before I knew it, this tiny hand was reaching out for mine. First time I'd ever shaken hands and rubbed noses with a King. It felt weird. I was glad when it was over. The opening ceremony for Mahinarangi was carried out with prayers, followed by speeches from the many dignitaries that were present – then the celebrations began.

Many performing groups participated as darkness fell. When we left, the celebrations were still in full swing. We arrived in Omaio late in the evening but Pop and I never stayed. We went straight back to Ratanui Station out of Tikitiki, which was a 2000 acre mixed farming property owned by my parents. It was shearing season, and the place was a hive of activity. Because it was the Christmas Holidays, there were a lot of children as well as the shearing gang.

My big sister Cissy was the cook for the shearing gang. She took over the kitchen. I always enjoyed spending time with Cissy and her children. When they were young they would keep us entertained. Cissy was a great cook. I worked in the shed as a fleeco and I enjoyed that. My mother taught me how to throw the fleece onto the table. There was a knack to this, which I soon mastered. My mother was also an A grade wool classer and took part in the Golden Shears in her day. I looked forward to smoko in the shed. Cissy would send two huge trays of her homemade scones, cakes or fried bread. They never lasted long. Breakfast, lunch and dinner were always at the house.

> Kiri had a wonderful experience as a member and part of a team for the television programme, Nga Kaka Wahanui (debating team).

I loved going to Ratanui, especially at Christmas, because all the family would come back for the holidays. Hiwi, Bess and their family; August, his wife Ruth and their family. August, Ruth and Hiwi were school teachers and had all moved away to follow their professions so school holidays gave everyone the opportunity to see family who lived far from home. My sister Taina and I used to quietly sneak into August and Ruth's bedroom early in the morning and take their baby John out of his cot and put him in our bed. We did this with Hiwi and Bessie's babies too. The children loved Ratanui. They dammed up the little creek so they could swim in it. They rode on the bikes with their uncles, and would do anything to ride the horses. They liked looking for eggs. Passionfruit vines grew wild through the pine trees at Ratanui. All we had to do was to spread pine needles on the ground and come back to find the fallen passionfruit.

A report in the Shout Radio newsletter (July 1997);

Introducing Kiri Atawhai Dewes a leader and supporter of community music in the Maori community.

Kiri is a fluent speaker in English and Maori. She is one of the original instigators of Victoria's State Body for Maori People, also known as the Polynesian Community Federation of Victoria (Te Rangatahi)... for future generations.

Kiri's knowledge of Maori culture is broad, achieving a Hiranga Certificate in Maori Studies and has a Bachelor of Arts degree in Social Science and Maori Studies. She is currently the cultural advisor to the National Museum of Victoria's Pacific Advisory Group, lectures in all aspects of Maori studies and the national and regional level judge of Maori cultural competitions in New Zealand and Australia. Kiri also has an interest in counselling from a Maori perspective, particularly dealing with youth problems and encouraging the teaching of music...

By Margaret Maru (Community Music Victoria's Music development Officer).

There were two orchards and Mum and Pop had muscovies, bantams, poultry, ducks, a pig called Punky, and a milking cow called Mooloo. There was a lovely vegetable garden that was lovingly tended by Father Bear, my Dad's stepfather. His name was Sam Tuau. He was Father Bear to all of us, and we loved him. He also took care of the mowing and the flower gardens.

In front of the house was a tennis court. It was flanked by my mother's beds of prize winning dahlias, and a lily pond. The Tikitiki Young Farmers Club used to come out to the farm and prune the fruit trees, and do some voluntary work on the farm as part of their training. My brothers, who were living on the farm then, were Lou, Cass and Tipuna. They all had motorbikes and I can remember learning to ride on Cass's motorbike. He had an Indian motorcycle and it was maroon.

From the homestead, the road gradually went down to the Maraehara River, which was just below the homestead. I went for a ride on the motorbike, crossed the river, and crashed into Sid Haig's gate. I put the brakes on but they were wet from crossing the river and I smashed through the gate. Cass wasn't happy, neither was Sid Haig. Luckily he liked me, because I used to catch eels for him, so he let me off.

I remember when I was still at high school, I'd go to Ratanui for the holidays. My brother's would pay me half a crown to iron their pants and shirts so they could go to the movies in Tikitiki. Pop had two trucks - a ute and a Morris, which was a bigger truck. They'd ask Mum for the ute but she'd say no, then they would send me to ask Pop, and he would give me the keys. Of course, they had to take me, as that was part of the deal.

At that time, my parents owned another farm, called Rauponga. It was closer to Tikitiki and from where the vehicles were parked near the house, it was an upward climb to the main road. The motor and lights were left off in case Mum would hear or she would stop us from going. My job was easy. It's amazing where you get the energy from when you need to. Once we got to the main road, my brother Lou would get me to move in between him and Cass, then he'd start the motor, switch on the lights, and away we'd go, with my other brother on the back of the truck. I went with them to concerts, dances and anything else that was going on in Tikitiki.

The end of the school holidays came all too soon. I had spent the last week with Mum in Te Horo. It was always hard leaving her. I hated leaving her, because when I took a sneaky look back through the rear vision mirror, I could see her crying. Gone were the days when Mum and I used to climb the hill to look for tawhara for Pop, when he was sick, or go eeling or whitebaiting. Thinking about it makes me choke back the tears. I never had a car so my biological father came and drove me to Hicks Bay.

I had the weekend to settle in at Hiwi's, and back to work on Monday for my first day at Hicks Bay School. Even though Hiwi and Bessie lived in the school house, Hiwi was teaching at Te Araroa High School and caught the bus each day to work. I had already met my new Principal, Mr Prosser, at Hiwi's so he introduced me to the rest of the staff. His wife, Mrs Prosser was the infant mistress then there was Jean Herewini and Maggie Kururangi. I had a good working relationship with them all.

Jean's Dad owned the local taxi, and Jean drove for him after work and weekends. Sometimes she used to pick me up for company. I remember one time we had to pick up a parcel from the bus depot in Te Araroa and deliver it to a home near the Hicks Bay wharf. Jean knew what was in the parcel but I didn't. She asked me to go in and get it, so I did. It was quite a long and heavy parcel, and as I tilted it, to put on the back seat, the end of the parcel broke and out fell this artificial leg onto the road. It was from the hip down. I got such a fright. By this time Jean was in fits of laughter. I refused to touch it so Jean picked it up and laid it on the back seat of the car. Anyway, we delivered it to the owner and I was always on my guard with Jean after that.

We had some great times together. Maggie and I played hockey for the Bay every weekend in Te Araroa. The Fish and Chip shop there was always popular after the games, especially for their kumara chips. Maggie and I became good friends and did a lot together. She married that year and moved to live with her husband. I never saw her again till she was a grandmother and living in Opotiki. I completed a year at Hicks Bay School.

In February the following year, I got married to George Dewes of Hicks Bay, and we moved to live in Waihaha in Western Lake Taupo with his brother Toke, his wife Francis and their family.

Life was very different. Francis and I stayed home, and George and Toke were fencing contractors for Lands and Survey. We were thirty-five miles from the nearest town, Mangakino. The roads were dirt and muddy in the wet weather and winter. In these times, all vehicles had to have chains around the tyres.

Most of the people that lived there were all working for Lands and Survey. A lot of them were breaking in the land for farming. There was a Farm Manager on this property. George and his brother were the fencers, and the rest of the men broke in the land. There was a camp of 150 men and only three women; the manager's wife, Francis, and I. The bridges were two logs laid across the rivers and streams. It was scary when there was frost or ice. We hardly had any contact with the outside world except when we went to Mangakino.

On the 27th of October, 1957, I gave birth to my first child, Wayne Tamahori Dewes who weighed 8lbs 2 ounces. No wonder I looked like a bloated terakihi when I was carrying him. He was my pride and joy. After his birth we went back to Ratanui for a year, and then George got a job as a shepherd on Mangatarata Station, a few miles out of Tokomaru Bay, so we moved there. It was quite lonely. If I didn't have my baby I would have gone nuts.

In those days there was no television, just the radio, so after I'd done all my household chores I'd pack some things for my baby into our little Vauxhall Wyvern. I would drive down to spend the day with my sister and her family in Waima, just out of Tokomaru Bay, and take her some mutton and eggs from the farm. We always had meat and eggs supplied free with the job and that was good.

Wayne was two years old when I had my next child. We were still living on the station. It was a really low time in my life. My baby was born in the Waipiro Bay Maternity Hospital but she was still-born. I wanted her so much. They placed her in my arms and she looked as if she was sleeping. It was so hard to let her go. She is buried in her father's family cemetery in Waipiro Bay. Mum asked me to give my baby her name, so she was named Riwia Moeroa, after my beloved Mum.

> Kiri wrote for the Learning Media in Wellington, NZ, where her work was used in many schools.

After the death of my daughter, I didn't want to be there anymore, so later that year we moved back to Western Lake Taupo. Meanwhile, Toke and Francis were in the process of having a house built in Taupo, and when that was completed they moved to Taupo, and we moved to Taurewa on a farm owned by Lands and Survey. George continued fencing for them.

Our nearest neighbours were a mile away at Kapoor's Mill. They were made up of two families. The Baker's and the Seymour's. There were three Baker brothers; Ted, Jim, and Gilbert, a sister, Liz, their partners and their families. They were Bushmen and mill workers, and often visited us in the evenings. We became good friends with these people. They had a few teenage children, and quite a few school age children as well. They had a little one-teacher school there, and the teacher was the only one that wasn't related.

We stayed till our son was nearly three years old, then bought our first house in National Park so we would be close to a school for him. We moved into our home early in 1959. It was good to have a home of our own at last. After we settled in, George got a job as a Prison Warden at Waikune Prison, a few miles down the road, whilst still working part time for Lands and Survey.

Judith Anne was born in Taumarunui Maternity Hospital on November 17th, 1959. I was overjoyed to have my precious little daughter, especially after losing my first baby girl. She was such a welcome addition to our family.

I honour the place in you in which the entire
universe resides. I honour the place in you,
which is of love, truth, light and of peace. I am
in that place in me, we are one.

Living in National Park was a lot different from where I grew up. We lived four miles from the mountains, namely: Tongariro, Ruapehu and the active mountain Ngauruhoe, so the climate was a lot colder. In winter, we had a lot of snow and some days we were knee deep in it. I remember having to dig the snow away from our foot paths and our garage door because the snow was so high. Some of the dads had to clear the paths to the school so the children could attend. The Ministry of Works was kept busy clearing the roads with graders and shovels.

It was dangerous driving after a snowfall because the roads were too slippery. Usually, only logging trucks and four-wheel drive vehicles were game enough to venture out on the highways. When it snowed at night, it left an awesome sight to see in the morning. It was white everywhere. The fences were half buried in snow, the trees were sagging with snow, and sometimes the huskies would come down from the mountains. I remember once in Taurewa, Ngauruhoe erupted, and the lava flow on the mountain was so bright you could see clearly at night.

While living there, we experienced heat at its worst and cold at its worst. Hailstones as big as eggs came down once and damaged a lot of cars, windows and buildings. Despite all this, I have many happy memories of my years there.

National Park is a small but well-known area for its ski fields, and slopes on Mount Ruapehu and Mount Ngauruhoe. Skiing enthusiasts from all over the world come to these mountains. It had a milk bar, grocer, butcher, post office, hotel, three timber mills, two service stations, and a railway station, so it was a busy little place.

We spent eleven years in National Park, and over that time, I did a few different things in this community. I was

National Park basketball team

elected onto the Tuwharetoa Tribunal for the area. This was a sensitive position for me because we were dealing with people's lives. These were Maori people who were in trouble with the law. If it was murder or something serious, the case went to court – anything else was usually handled by the tribunal. The punishment was given and the offender or offenders were present. They all knew who we were, and I'd get a dirty look whenever they saw me. However, when it concerned neglected children, abused or beaten wives, I had no difficulty in raising my hand. Most punishments were probation, home after a certain time, abstaining from alcohol, or community work.

I also trained as a Cub leader for the area because my son Wayne loved being a part of the pack. I was selected to take the Cub packs from the Waimarino District to see Lady Baden Powell in Auckland. That was a real high for me. My friend Cilla Te Oriki came and helped with the boys. We took up two carriages on the train and the children loved the whole experience, the train, and seeing Lady Baden Powell.

I was twenty-three when I took the group to meet Lady Baden-Powell. Another time we also met the Queen Mother when she came to Ohakune in 1963. This was a memorable event for us as she was driven onto the field in an open topped Land Rover. When she got off and walked along the different scout groups, cubs, girl guides, and brownies of the Waimarino District, she shook hands with many of the youngsters. I got the shock of my life when she stopped to talk to me – all I could rustle up was a nod and smile at her (there was a photo of the Queen Mother and I on a magazine, but we never kept a copy).

Later, after one of the Royals visited New Zealand, Mount Ruapehu erupted and the boiling water from the top of the mountain overflowed into the Tangiwai River, just out of Ohakune, and swept away a passing train, killing all the passengers. All the dead were laid out on the street in Ohakune, and relatives came from miles around to try to identify and claim their dead. The wailing could be heard for quite a distance.

The Great Forest of Tane

I sit beside a waterfall in the Great forest of Tane
And drink in the beauty of all that surrounds me
I listen intently to the medley of sounds
That echo within this place so sublime
The rushing sound of the falls that cascade
Form an eddying pool in the river below
I remember the feats that Tane accomplished
How he clothed his mother laying prone below
Covered her nakedness with plants and trees
Then created the animals, insects and birds
Creatures as well to dwell and survive
In this domain so clean and so free
Walk in the forest, stay awhile, be still
Listen to the sound of the rustling leaves
The whispering winds, the shuffle of creatures
The music of songbirds, the stillness of night
The whirring and buzz of busy insects
This special place, this paradise
Where I find peace and comfort
A haven to reflect on the past
And dream of the future.

This was known as the Tangiwai Disaster. Every time back then when Royalty visited New Zealand there was a major disaster. The Waitangi Disaster, The Tangiwai Disaster, The Kaimai Disaster are some that happened not long after a Royal visit.

In 1961 I gave birth to my beautiful baby girl, Shelley Rose. When I was carrying her, I was knitting a little jacket ready for her arrival, and the name of the pattern was "Shelley", so that is how she got her first name. The second part of her name, 'Rose', was after a dear friend of mine, who lived in Auckland. She was part of the Baker family from Kapoor's Mill. Two years later I had another son called Kenneth Rex. He was named by my Aunt Paul, after two Mormon Elders who spent several months staying with her. When my baby was three months old, I lost him. He died in the Taumarunui Hospital. The doctor said he had contracted pneumonia. I remember that morning too well. About six o'clock I could hear him stirring in his bassinet so I reached out and placed him in bed with me. He was breast fed, and I cuddled him into me while he was on my breast. It was snug and warm. When he went back to sleep, I tucked him up in his cuddly rug, and laid him back in his bassinet. As I was awake, I got up to do my washing, and get it out on the line, and do other daily chores before he awoke so I could be with him.

Translator

Kiri, worked as a translator, of English to Maori, or Maori to English. She translated the book *Lion King* into Maori, as she did a few other well-known books.

It is not wrong to cry or want attention. It is not even wrong to scream or throw a tantrum. What is wrong is to keep it inside, and punish yourself simply for being human.

I checked him regularly. By 9.30, I thought he'd been asleep long enough so I picked him up and touched his cheek. My fingers made imprints in his cheeks. I laid him down to change his diaper and my hands left marks on his skin. I panicked, and lifted him up, his eyes were rolling and would not stay open. I rang the nurse but she did not answer her phone. I rang the police, and they went around to the nurse – she was doing book work and not answering her phone. She came over with the police, where my baby and I got into her car and drove to Taumarunui Hospital. I left my other children with my friend Rose, and her family who had moved from Kapoor's Mill to Taylors' Mill in Taumarunui, so that was handy. I was with my baby all day at the hospital. I couldn't contact George because I didn't know where he was, and of course, mobile phones weren't invented then.

My baby was put into a humidicrib, and I could see his little chest rising up and down so fast. His little eyes kept following me whenever I moved around the humidicrib. About 9.30 that night the doctor suggested that I go home and rest and they would keep me informed if there was any change. So I went back to my other children at the Baker's home and they were waiting for me. I sat in their lounge, no one wanted to sleep, so we sat talking.

Right on the hour of midnight there was knock on the door. I knew at once that it was the police. They came to tell me my precious little son had passed away. I was a mess. I kept asking myself what I had done to deserve this. Immediately, George was on the phone to our families in Gisborne to tell them we were taking our baby home to lie with his sister in Waipiro Bay. Our friend, Ted Baker and his family in his car; Toke, Francis and their family in their Land Rover and George, me, and our family in our Land Rover, we all set out to Gisborne after we had picked our baby up in Taumarunui. By the time we reached the Waioeka Gorge, the rain was coming down in torrents. The men had to chop away a tree that had fallen across the road and dig away a slip as well. We were lucky to get through the gorge that night.

We arrived at George's Mum's home in Lyndhurst Street at about three in the morning. We brought the baby into the lounge. My children and I slept with our baby. Early that morning I could hear loud wailing and I knew it was my big sister. I was so relieved to have her there because I never had any of my immediate family with me. I was to share my grief with her. I couldn't wait to leave this place as I felt uncomfortable there. We finally left about 11.00 am and arrived in Waipiro Bay about 1.30 pm. All my family was there, and my baby was laid to rest with his sister that afternoon.

I left with a heavy heart. We drove back to Gisborne that afternoon and spent the night with my sister. The next morning we all went back to the King Country.

During this time, my nephew Coby had come to live with us. He was my sister Cissy's eldest child but was raised by my maternal grandfather. He acquired a job in the Tongariro Timber Mill in National Park and was happy there. Sometimes he worked on the fence line with George on weekends. He was such fun to have around. He had a great sense of humour and was a big hit with the local females, much to his delight.

My youngest brother Patrick was a student at St. Stephens College in Auckland. He always came to us for the school holidays, and to work in the mill for pocket money. When it was time to go back to college he didn't want to go. I encouraged him to go back and reluctantly he did. He loved coming to us for his holidays.

Even though National Park was a small place, there was always something on for the young people on the weekends, such as dances, concerts, skiing, pig hunting and deer stalking. In 1962, Wayne started school. His first day was the hardest. He didn't want to go, so I had to practically drag him to school. I stayed awhile with him till he settled. In those days teachers were scarce so I started relieving at the school. I took my children with me to work and they loved it. My son was happier knowing I was there. It wasn't easy being a wife, a mother, and teaching, but the extra money came in handy and I managed to cope with it all.

I now had three children; Wayne, Judy and Shelley. Judy was three and Shelley was one, and we all went to school. Sometimes I worked for months until they could get a permanent teacher, but I was always on call and that was okay.

My life was really busy with my babies, my work with the Cubs and working with the Maori Tribunal; I also took Maori Club at the scout hall once a week. Every Thursday evening I would drive twenty-eight miles into Taumarunui and teach adult classes the Maori language. Our Maori Club in National Park was well known in the surrounding communities. Different places would hold field days, sport days and rodeos. One of the events of the day was where the Culture Clubs competed for trophies and our club used to collect all the major prizes.

Cub Mistress

A lot of the people and children who lived in National Park had never seen the sea, therefore we ran a few concerts and fundraisers, and I took our club and some of their parents on a bus trip to Te Araroa on the East Coast. The club had ladies hockey teams and a rugby team. I let our hosts in Te Araroa know because it was the Tokorarangi Hockey and Rugby Club hosting us.

We left early on a Saturday morning and arrived in Te Araroa fairly late in the afternoon. As we drove along the coastal roads, the children were so excited to see the sea. The bus driver was great with the children and stopped a few times to give them a stretch and let them paddle in the sea. We made sure to stop at the beach and to have the lunch that was prepared by the mothers, hence our late arrival in Te Araroa.

Our accommodation for the week was on Tokorarangi Marae, an awesome experience for the children, especially the sleeping in the ancestral building. Every chance they got they were down to the beach. Our hosts looked after us, and it was good to taste a lot of home cooking. There was fresh seafood every day. I don't remember who won all the games but I'll never forget the hospitality given to us by the Tokorarangi Club of Te Araroa. On our final night with them, our club put on a concert. Many people from the neighbouring settlements came. A silver coin was taken at the door and the proceeds were given to our hosts.

The morning we left there were floods of tears because our children had made new friends in this little settlement, so the parting for them was sad. I knew a lot of them would never be in this place again, and that it was totally different from where they came from. However, I knew they would not forget that visit for a long time.

I also took them on a visit to the Waitomo Caves. We had a guide who took us on boats through the underground river in the caves. The glow worms were a sight to behold. We had to be quiet, otherwise their lights would go off. As the guide steered us through the caves, the sounds of the water dripping from the ceiling was like music to listen to. Inside the caves are several limestone formations and there is a place that is called 'The Cathedral.' Famous singers, like Inia Te Wiata, Kiri Te Kanawa, and many others have sung there. My little troopers sang there too. They sang their rendition of *Nearer my God to Thee* and the acoustics in this magical space were awesome. Our trip there was a day trip, but it was a memorable day for me, as well as the children.

The Wonder of it all

I've often sat and wondered why
I had to go away
At the age of seven months
with my aunt to stay
I look back now and understand
why it had to be
You see I do believe
that it was meant to be
It was all a part of the Creators perfect plan
I learnt so much throughout the years
The songs and chants and tales of old
The stories that the old folks told
The medicines, the food and more
Provided by Mother Nature's store
And now I'm in my senior years
And have a family of my own
Five generations down
I'm so proud of my children, grandchildren, great grandchildren too

And I am truly blessed to add three great, great
grandchildren too.
They are my precious pride and joy
They mean the world to me
I realise now why it was that I had to be
With my aunt who was my Mum
She loved me, flaws and all
I have a treasure trove of memories
too precious to forget
She was the greatest Mum to me
and I have no regrets.
I know she watches over me in everything I do
and I'm so blessed and lucky for the family I have
too.

Alone in my home one day, I was thinking of my Mum and so decided to pen my thoughts.

MY LIFE STORY – PART 3

Mum often came to visit and I loved having her. She would stay for a month just to be with us.

I know it was too cold for her but we always had both our open fires going in our living room and our lounge. Central heating wasn't heard of then, but wood was plentiful, so keeping our house warm was no problem. There was plenty of wood from the mills and logs from the forests.

My Aunty Paul visited often. She worked in the Tikitiki Waiapu Farmers for years. I remember when I was young and went to Tikitiki, I used to stand at the door of the shop where she worked and when she'd spot me she would give me a real angry look and ask me in her grumpy voice, "What are you doing here?" And I'd say, "Nothing", and she'd throw me three pence, and say, "Now get out of my sight". I'd take off with my three pence. It doesn't mean much today but I could do wonders with three pence back then.

Anyway, whenever she had a break she would come to National Park and I'd reminisce with her and remind her how grumpy she used to be and how when we lived in Whakawhitira she used to ride her bicycle about nine miles from Tikitiki to our house in Whakawhitira. Our house was across the Mangaoporo River and we could spot her on the other side of the river. We would dread her arrival because she was so gruff and always had this real mean look about her, yet really, she wasn't mean. Anyway, I loved reminding her of how mean she was to us when we were kids growing up. Despite all this, I loved my aunt and enjoyed her visits with us.

Tikitiki

Taumarunui was the closest town church from us so we always went there to do our shopping. One time my biological parents came to visit us with Aunty Paul, and we took them to Mount Ruapehu where the ski fields were. Of course, they were fascinated with the chair lifts that carried people from the base of the mountain to the village and ski fields high up on the mountain.

To enter the chair lift, you backed in to a chair, and it scooped you up and took you up the mountain. Naturally, you had to pay before catching the lift. Mum and Aunt were already swaying along in their seats when they remembered Pop. They shouted to him, "Come on Pop" but poor old Pop didn't have any money because Mum always carried it. The lift operator wouldn't let him on, so he had to walk. Well, Pop thought he'd fix those women up for leaving him behind so he made his own way up the mountain. When the ladies came down from the mountain I was waiting for them.

We waited and waited for Pop, and Mum was really starting to worry. At last we spotted him sauntering along towards us. We were so relieved. Mum asked him where he had been and he said, "Well, you two left me behind so I decided to make my own way up the mountain. I stopped and had a wash in a stream. Then I met a friendly Irishman and we went up and down the mountain together. Pop was carrying what was left of his sandals in his hand. There were no soles left on them. My poor Pop. He made my mother find a shoe repairer to mend his sandals and after quite a search she found someone who repaired them. He was happy with the result.

My father was such a special person to me. He was highly respected by many, a genius in Maori oratory, and a father that I wouldn't trade for the world. He was wise yet humble. There are so many things I remember and love him for. Seldom is there a day when I don't think of him. At this time I was still living in the King Country in National Park, which is twenty-eight miles North West of Taumarunui. There are a few settlements between, namely: Raurimu, Oio, Owhango, Piriaka and Manunui.

Raurimu is famous for its 'Spiral', which is the only rail line in the world that crosses over itself twice underground before it reaches the top of the hill in National Park. You could hear it chugging slowly as it climbed the spiral. If you were catching the train south, you had plenty of warning and time to get to the station. My two nieces who lived in Wellington came up to see us often on long weekends. They were both working in Wellington but would turn up every now and then.

I loved having my relatives visit, and missed them when they left. My brother August and his wife, Ruth, would come every school holidays and spend a couple of days with us. Then they would leave their three children and come for them at the end of the holidays. As soon as they would see their parents car arrive, they all ran and hid. Their parents would call and they wouldn't answer. Their father would say, "Okay, come out or you won't come here again." They would come out, and lips would be hanging. Their father would give them a hug and all was okay.

I had a very close relationship with all my nieces and nephews, and over the years it has not diminished. I adore every one of them. I remember back in the early sixties, we were the only house that had television. When the local children heard, we would have a house full of children watching our television. The snow on the TV was as big as eggs but that didn't stop them coming. We put cellophane paper over the screen and that made it a little clearer. It was better than nothing in those days. The reception wasn't very clear because the closest transformer to us was on the other side of Taihape, many miles away. By the time the reception was good, nearly every house had a TV.

Taumarunui was a quiet town. I took my Aunty Paul there for the first time and after driving through the main street, then walking and window shopping, she said "This town reminds me of the places you see in the Wild West movies". I suppose it was because the buildings were so old. She saw all these people walking down a path from the main street to the back street and pointing, she asked, "Where are all those people going?" I replied, "They are going to the Social Security Office to collect their pensions". It was the end of the shearing season there and all the shearing gangs were in to collect their fortnightly pensions and benefits.

The main street of Taumarunui had the shops on one side and the Railway Station and Parks on the other. The little café at the railway station sold the best coffee and hot chocolate. Magnolias graced the park the full length of the main street, and when they were in bloom, it was a sight to behold. The park was a place where people gathered after shopping. Some to rest, read, eat or just relax.

Taumarunui also had the only hospital for miles around. Four of my children were born there. In those days you were not allowed out of your bed for three days and you were not permitted to leave the hospital till the tenth day after the birth. If the baby's umbilical cord had not come off you stayed. Times have changed so much since then. It had its advantages in that it gave the mother a well-deserved rest. Children weren't allowed in the wards and that made me sad.

All I could do was stand at the window and wave to my children standing on the lawn below with their Dad. I could hear them calling, "Hi Mummy!" All I wanted to do was pick them up and hug them. I hated watching them leave. We weren't even allowed to have our babies with us except at feeding time. My heart sank whenever the nurse came to take my baby back to the nursery. The days seem to drag when you're in there, until finally, you go home with your new bundle of joy and everyone is happy and life goes on. Now we had Wayne, Judy, Shelley and Patrick.

Towards the end of 1966, my children and I moved back to Gisborne to be near my Mum, who had had several heart attacks. I wanted to be there for her. George stayed back in National Park and continued working at Waikune Prison until the sale of our home in National Park was finalised. Meanwhile, my children and I moved in with my biological parents for a couple of months. I then rented a property in Palmerston Road. Aunty Paul moved in with us. Patrick was my baby, and my aunt cared for him during the day, while I went back teaching in a relieving capacity. My three older children were attending Gisborne Central School. This was right in the city, and close to our home.

My Shelley was in my class and she was so funny. She refused to call me Mum or Miss; instead, she would always come up and tap me on the shoulder or stand behind me and give me a sneaky pinch on the butt.

It was good to get back teaching after so long. I met one of my friends one day when I was up the street, and she was teaching. She told me of a vacancy at Gisborne central School so I applied and got the position. From there, I relieved in other local schools including Gisborne Intermediate School, Awapuni Primary School and Gisborne Girls High School.

George came back to Gisborne three months after us. We soon bought a block of land to build on. This was near the airport. We planned to build a cottage at the back of the house for Mum but by now her health had deteriorated and she passed away on the 4th of August, 1967. That was the biggest blow to my life, even though in my heart I knew it was a welcome release for her. She was seventy-two years old so she had a good innings. I was four months pregnant with my last baby and it was hard for me to accept that she was really gone. At the burial I was not allowed to go onto the cemetery as that is an absolute no-no to my people when you are pregnant. I really struggled with that.

After Mum's death, I no longer wanted to build our house on the section that we had bought so we sold it and bought another section on the main street close to town. It wasn't long and our house was ready for us to move into. On February the 12th, my baby girl Christine Margaret was born in Cook Hospital. Her father was at work at Wattie's Cannery and I didn't have time to ring him to come home and take me to the hospital so my neighbour David Marino came and took me. I nearly had my baby at home so I just made it to the hospital.

I joined the Apostolic Church and found peace there after my Mum's death. I had all my children dedicated in that church.

It was at this time that my marriage was on the way out. Things were not the same between us anymore, and I didn't want my children to see us like that. I tried to make him come to church with me but he wouldn't. There was a lot of personal stuff going on between us that only he and I knew of. I felt I couldn't share this with anyone.

One morning after a confrontation with him, I knew I couldn't go on like this any longer. I waited until he went to work, then I got my children together and told them I was leaving their Dad and that I wanted to take them with me. However, I think they really knew what was going on and they told me they didn't want to come with me. I had put a lot of thought into the situation and as much as I wanted to take my children with me, all I knew at that time was that I had to leave. I think my children thought I would come back but in my heart I knew I would not.

I packed a bag and when my children went to school, I caught a plane to Auckland. It was the hardest thing for me to leave my children but I knew I had to go. I took my baby who was eighteen months old at the time and my daughter Shelley. We spent the night in Auckland. The following day we caught the train to Christchurch in the South Island and stayed with a friend of mine for two days. I then got a rental house close to the city and the Avon River. I had a sister staying in Christchurch who looked after my baby when I was at work. My baby's namesake, Christine, stayed with us, and we both found work in Mary Potter Hospital. I worked as a nurse and Christine worked as a cleaner. It was really hard as I missed my children so much.

Back in Gisborne I was more or less an outcast to most of my relatives. They drew their own conclusions about why I left my children but no one knew the truth, only George and I. I did write a letter to my father explaining why I left, and in my heart, I know he understood. So I moved on but kept busy – nursing during the day from 7.00 am till 3.00 pm, and cleaning offices for 'The Christchurch Star', a newspaper firm in the evenings. These were both Monday to Friday jobs. On Saturdays and Sundays I worked in a nursing home, so my days were full, but that's the way I wanted it, so as to keep my mind occupied. It wasn't easy.

In my heart I knew that one day my children would ask me why I left them and I would tell them the truth, and whether they believe it or not is up to them. I would never turn them against their father. What happened was between him and me. I know if I had stayed, I wouldn't be here today.

I was a member of the Apostolic Church in my home town and often accompanied the pastor on many of his missions to people. When he heard I had left my husband, he came to Christchurch to ask me to go home with him to George. But I knew the situation between George and I was beyond repair, and so I remained in Christchurch. My Aunty Paul brought my children to spend the school holidays with me and it was great seeing and having them with me. I know they had accepted that I wasn't going home and that made it easier. It was always hard letting them go home, yet I knew they were better off in their own home.

I spent three years in Christchurch. One year nursing at Mary Potter Hospice and two years at Christchurch Women's Hospital, working night shift in the Central Sterilising Department. I worked alone autoclaving circumcision packs for new born babies. I enjoyed my work there and I learnt a lot. It was a responsible job and I had to make sure each pack prepared was exact.

It was while I was working there that I received a letter from my niece Celia, informing me that she was dying of cancer in Wellington Hospital. I was very fond of my niece so I decided to move back to Wellington so that I could be with her. At the same time, Aunty Paul came down and asked me to let her take my two daughters,

My Precious One

Huriana, my precious one
Don't ever rest content
On your mountains' gentle slopes
But conquer every summit
And tread the sacred trails
Of your ancestors
Your forebears
Fill your baskets with the wisdom
and lore of the Maori and the white man
So that you will never falter in this ever changing world.

Here I am speaking to my granddaughter, expressing my thoughts to her on the trails I would like her to take as she journeys through life. That she should not linger at the lower levels of education, but to ascend to the highest peaks of learning in both worlds, so that she can stand proud and strong in the days ahead.

Shelley and Christine, back home to Gisborne with her. As much as I wanted to keep them, I knew they would be better off with the rest of my children in their own home so I agreed.

After they left, I felt so alone and when I received my niece's letter, I packed and moved back to Wellington. I stayed at the 'Peoples Palace', which was not far from the hospital. I visited my niece every day for two weeks, then I went to stay with a cousin in Strathmore and got a job at Interlock Industries. This was walking distance from where I lived. I bought myself a little Triumph Herald car while I was working there. I loved it. My niece passed away shortly after I moved in with my cousin. It was quite odd. I had just stepped into the house after work and I felt something brush past me so I looked behind me and I saw Celia by the door but just for a moment, and I knew she had passed away. Shortly after the phone rang. It was my sister telling me that Celia had died. By now some of the family knew that I was in Wellington.

I attended my niece's funeral and, of course, all the family was there. I don't know what their thoughts were but I know I was there for my niece. I always had a close relationship with my brother Hiwi and his wife Bessie. They always kept in touch with me and let me know what was going on back home. I loved them dearly for they never judged me, nor asked me any questions, but always told me they loved me.

One day, not long after Celia's death my forelady at work told me there was a tall, dark, handsome gentleman at the front desk to see me. I went there and was shocked to see my father standing in the doorway. I was lost for words and just stood there. He took off his hat and hugged me. He was such a gentleman. No words passed between us for some time and we just stood there hugging each other. By now, I was in tears, and memories were flashing through my mind. I remember my last meeting with our father before I left. He was angry with me because he saw an advertisement in the local paper where I had my car for sale. He wanted to know why I was selling it, and to tell him why I was leaving.

After some time he asked me if I would have dinner with him as he was staying in Wellington for a couple of days. I agreed, and after work went to Lower Hutt, where we had dinner at a local restaurant. He told me he received my letter and that he understood. That was the last time I saw my father alive. I adored him in life, and even in death he is an inspiration. I just need to think of him and I'm inspired, especially when I'm writing. He passed away a year after my birth mother died. I know he missed her so much. Anyway, I have many happy memories of my beloved father.

Life continued, and I moved on and got a job at the Wellington Airport, working in the restaurant. That was a new experience for me. I found it rewarding and met a lot of people. I learnt a lot while I was there. I stayed there for a year, then moved to a little two room cottage in Petone, and worked at Southward Motors and General Motors on the assembly lines for a while. I also worked as a barmaid, then as travelling saleswoman for Tenderkist Meats. This was a job that I really enjoyed. I travelled the Hutt Valley, Wellington, Newlands, Johnsonville, Tawa, Porirua, Porirua East, Titahi Bay, Plimmerton, Pukerua Bay, Paekakariki, Paraparaumu, right through to Waikanae, delivering their smallgoods.

A while later my youngest brother Patrick was killed in Australia. I was doing deliveries in the Tawa-Johnsonville area, when my boss called me on the intercom and told me to come back to the factory immediately. I was shocked because he told me it was Pat; I didn't know if it was my brother or my son, as they were both named Pat. It wasn't till I got back to the factory that I found out it was my baby brother. I was so upset and I made up my mind to go to Australia and bring my brother home.

My boss gave me a month's leave and I was grateful for that. I drove out to my big sister's home in Taita, and my parents were there. I rang Australia and spoke to my brother's friends. They pleaded with me to leave my brother in Australia and they would take care of everything regarding the funeral. So it was agreed by my family that my younger sister and I would fly to Melbourne, Australia to attend my brother's funeral.

He was twenty-nine years old when he and his girlfriend were tragically killed in a car train collision in Kensington, a suburb of Melbourne. He had a great send off and by the attendance at his funeral, I know he was loved by many. There were so many people they couldn't all fit into the church, so some went ahead and waited at the cemetery. Pat was a member of a band called PJ's and they were the resident band at the New Anglers Hotel in Maribyrnong where he lived and worked as a barman. His death brought me to Australia for the first time.

Publisher's Note

At one time sitting with Kiri, she was playing with her iPad, and entered her name in one of those games where it describes the character of the owner. In this case, when talking about the name's owner being two-faced or not, it said; you are 0%. You're REAL! You never sugar coat your words because you know how hurtful lies can be. You'd rather give people the truth, brutally honest truth.

Kiri laughed about this, and said that there have been many times when she has upset people because of her brutal honesty. Anyone who knows Kiri will concur; that this is who she is.

MY LIFE STORY – PART 4

Patrick my brother

I remember boarding the plane at Rongopai Airport in Wellington with my younger sister. It was the first time we were to be out of New Zealand. All sorts of thoughts were running through my mind. I'd never been on a plane before; *I don't like heights, hope we don't crash, I can't swim; I don't think I'll have the guts to jump out of the plane if anything happens to it.* Anyway, I'm sitting in my seat with all these thoughts going through my mind and then I saw a hostess in the aisle just ahead of me. The voice over the speaker system started the demonstration air drill, about what we should do if we have to bail out of the plane. I froze. Oh my God, I couldn't hear a thing she was saying. The hostess doing the demonstration was just a blur. If the plane did run into difficulties I wouldn't know what to do.

The take-off was a nightmare. I never prayed so hard and while I was praying I kept hearing a still small voice in my head saying, "And when you call my name I will hear you not". My ears were tingling, my hands were aching from gripping onto the seat. When I finally opened my eyes we had levelled off in the air. I had a window seat, and when I looked out the window and saw the land below, I didn't feel too bad until we were over the sea, then nausea set in. If we did have to bail out over the sea I'd drown for sure because I could only dog paddle and that wouldn't get me far. It took me a while to settle down and relax. I guess it was the smell of food drifting down the aisle that took my mind off my fears for a while. After we had eaten I felt a little more relaxed about being up in the air. Three and half hours later we landed in Melbourne. That was scary too, especially when the wheels of the plane hit the ground and the brakes were applied. I was holding tight to my seat and applying my brakes too. I heaved a big sigh of relief when the plane finally stopped. After we'd gone through all the formalities and collected our bags, we worked our way to the front of the main building. When we got outside it was sweltering. It was cold when we left Wellington so we must have looked ridiculous all togged up in our winter gear.

We were met by two of my brother's friends and driven to the New Angler's Hotel in Maribyrnong. There were so many people there to greet us. They gave us my brother's suite for the duration of our stay. I felt at home in this space. There was a double bed, a single bed, and big fish tank. We couldn't wait to slip into something cooler, then went back to the lounge to socialise. The manager of the hotel was Patrick's friend, and he filled us in on how my brother was killed, as well as the details regarding the funeral service and the burial. He asked us if we would like to view the body. I said no because he had already told my sister and I that we wouldn't recognise him as he was badly cut up. I wanted to remember him as I last saw him.

After dinner we were entertained by the other members of my brother's band until quite late in the evening then we returned to our suite. My sister refused to sleep in his bed so she had the single bed and I slept in my brother's double bed. I felt close to him in his bed. My sister was scared. When I switched off the light she said, "Hey! Switch the light back on." I switched the light back on and left it on all night.

The next morning after breakfast, we were driven in a Cadillac to St Thomas' Church in Moonee Ponds to attend the funeral service for my brother. The church was packed. My sister and I were ushered into the church by Roger Pitt, who was responsible for all the arrangements for the funeral. He took us right up to the casket, and as we stood there, I was aware that the eyes of the people were on us. This made it quite difficult for me to express my emotions and say farewell to my baby brother the way I would have liked to. I felt cheated because I couldn't see him or touch him, like we do in our culture. I had to remember I was in another country and their ways were different to ours. I was so close to him and yet so far. In fact, only a few inches separated us, but I couldn't touch him. I spoke my farewells softly to him, then my sister and I sat down. When the service ended, everyone followed the hearse to Fawkner cemetery for the burial service. We met his partner Beverley Fisher's mother and sister. The attendance at both the church and burial services showed us just how much he meant to so many.

After the service at the cemetery, everyone was invited back to the hotel for refreshments. That evening my brother's band dedicated the evening to my sister and me. They spoke about their experiences and memorable times with Patrick, and sang all their favourite songs. At the end of the evening, they changed the name of their band from 'PJ's' to 'Minus One.' I thought that was great. My sister and I stayed with Pat's friend, Roger Pitt, and his partner, the owners of The New Angler's Hotel for nine days, and in that time we met so many of Pat's friends and fans.

This place is so different to home. The pace is so much faster. My sister Taina and I thought we would go out on our own one day and see if we could find our way back to the hotel so we caught a tram that took us to Moonee

Ponds. We got off the tram in Puckle Street and wandered down the street looking in the shops that drew our interest. We bought a few things and had something to eat then went back to catch the tram to take us back to the hotel.

The rest of our stay at the New Angler's Hotel, and the people we befriended while there, will always remain precious memories to my sister and me. On our last night, we had dinner with so many of Pat's friends. Taina and I sang 'Pokarekare ana' for them. We retired about 1.00 am. The next morning, Roger and Ray Tawha, a friend of Pat's, took us to the airport. There were several others who were already there to bid us farewell with flowers and gifts for us. It was lovely. When we went through customs, they took away our flowers and that really annoyed me. However, we got through the rest of the formalities and wandered on down to the departure lounge and waited until we were asked to board our plane.

We boarded and sat in our seats then I started worrying again. Quietly, I said a little prayer, and asked that our guardian angels surround the plane, be with the pilot and passengers, and guide us safely back to our homeland, Aotearoa. I felt good after that but still held on to my seat at take-off until we were airborne. Even now, it still worries me every time the air drill demonstration is on, and I can't wait until the plane is on the ground again.

Freedom

I envy the wind as it blows free
Over the land and over the sea
Into the heavens in swoops and swirls
Sending the clouds in a frenzy of whirls
I envy the rain as it falls free
Into our waterways that flow to the sea
There to be tossed by Tangaroa's waves
Thrown to the shores and into the caves
No rules to bind them in any way
Just fancy free from day to day
So pure, so clean, so fresh and free
This is what freedom means to me.

I never asked my mother for much, just a slim body and a fat bank account. But I think she got them mixed up.

On arrival in Wellington, we were met by family and taken back to my eldest sister's home in Taita. Members of our family were waiting to hear about our journey to Australia for our brother's funeral. Every time I travel, I always take a journal and keep a record of events from the time we leave home until the time we return, so I had a record of everything that happened while we were in Australia. Dad was impressed. He told me he would send me anywhere in the world on his behalf.

On our return from Australia, I felt unsettled and had a deep pull to go back there to be close to my brother. I believe in my heart that it was time for me to move on. All sorts of thoughts and questions were brewing in my mind; *What about my children; my friends? Will I be happy there? Will I find work? Will I make it?* Anyway, I gave up with Tenderkist Meats and drove a taxi for Charlie Sheppard for ten months. I then bought if off him. The next year I returned to Australia in March for the anniversary of my brother's death. Every time I left home to go to Australia my cousin Anzac Te Maro would drive my taxi for me.

In 1975 I spent a month in Australia and I had my son Patrick with me for the duration. I was glad he was with me. He and I stayed in Westmeadows, with Greg and Beverly Pitt and their children, Murray, Troy and Jody. I will always remember this family with so much love and affection because they made my son and me so much a part of their family. My son was named after my brother Patrick. He was four months old when my brother left for Australia but I was proud that I named my son after him. He was eight years old when Patrick was killed.

I remember when my brother left Auckland airport. He climbed the steps of the plane to the top landing, looked back and waved to us. He had a big smile and looked so handsome in his black trousers, white shirt and royal blue blazer. This is how I will remember him always. That was the last time I saw him alive.

Early in January 1976, I decided to sell up and move to Australia. By March, I had tied up all my loose ends, sold my taxi, and left New Zealand, bound for Australia. All sorts of thoughts were occupying my mind as I sat in my seat on the plane.

Have I done the right thing by moving to Australia? Will I be happy? Will I find work, and will things work out in a positive way?

Anyway, I arrived at Melbourne Airport, then after collecting my luggage and going through customs, I was really happy to spot the drummer, Ken Smith, from my brother Pat's band, as I walked through the arrivals door. Both he and his wife Beverly were there to meet me. I was going to be staying with them till I sorted myself out.

I moved into a bungalow at the back of their house and was comfortable there. After a month, I went back to Petone in New Zealand and brought my eldest daughter Judy and her baby Shelley Jay back to Australia with me. Judy was very pregnant with her second child. We all stayed in the bungalow at Beverly and Ken's home in St Albans. By this time, my second eldest daughter, Shelley Rose joined us. Times were hard but we managed. We had a week to settle in to our house, shopping and making connections with people.

I started work in North Sunshine in a butcher's shop that was owned by a friend of my brother Pat. I loved it. I learned how to cure corned beef, how to make sausages, and run and serve in the shop. It was a great experience.

It was while I was working there that my daughter Judy gave birth to Kristel Paula in the Western General Hospital in Footscray. She had a lot of difficulty breathing when she was born and was transferred to the Royal Children's Hospital in Melbourne. After a few tests were run they found that she had two holes in her heart. That certainly was a worry for Judy, Shelley and I. They performed major heart surgery on her. She was a real battler. We spent three months travelling daily to the hospital. Judy stayed at the hospital as she was breast feeding, not only her baby, but a set of twins that were there as well. After three months we were able to take our bundle of joy home.

By this time I had decided to take a position as a barmaid at the St. Albans Hotel, which was more convenient for me, as it was closer to our home. The bar manager there was a friend of my brother's, so I was lucky to get work. This was a very busy hotel compared to the hotels I had worked in back in New Zealand. I worked in the public bar. There was four bartenders and the bar manager on duty each shift. There were two shifts, 10.00 am – 6.00 pm, and 6.00 pm – 1.00 am. There were eighteen pool tables in this bar and it was busy day and night. The clientele were predominantly European; Maltese, Macedonian, Greek, and of course the local Aussies. One would ask me for a pot and I would serve him a glass of port. He would say to me, "No, No! I want a pot of beer". So I had to familiarise myself with the different accents and words. In New Zealand they ask for a handle not a pot. It didn't take long for me to grasp the different accents and to get to know the regular customers by name and to know what they drank. We were so busy the time passed quickly and it was a welcome call from the boss when it was finishing time for us. For the first week, I couldn't wait to go home after work and get off my feet because I was on them from the time I started work until finishing time. There was no time to sit down.

It was quite funny sometimes at work, especially from Thursday to Sunday night. I'd be busy behind the bar and someone would say, "Kia ora", and I'd look up and see a Maori face or a white Kiwi smiling back at me, that always made me feel good. In fact, I soon found out that there were a few Maori families living in St Albans. I befriended a young Maori man named Chris Hurst from Te Kuiti. His wife Kathy worked as a barmaid with me. He was the leader of a band called 'Jedda Country'. They played Saturday evenings at the pub.

I bought a Volkswagen and that enabled Judy, Shelley and I to be more independent. I remember one time when we were driving to the hospital to see Judy and the baby – we were driving up a steep slope in Green Gully, when Shelly said, "Shame, Mum, that big truck is passing us uphill", and she ducked so the driver of the truck wouldn't see her.

Another time we were driving along Ballarat Road in Footscray. In the next lane, parallel to us, was a white ute with three guys sitting on the tray talking to each other and laughing. Shelley said, "Look, they're laughing at our car." I was sure they were laughing at their own jokes. Anyway, Shelley had a real thing about our car, yet there was nothing wrong with it. If anyone looked at us while we were out driving, she'd glare at them.

When our baby was three months old, Judy took her back to Gisborne and decided to stay there with her father. Shelley and I decided to move out of the house and I bought a twenty-eight foot Viscount Royal caravan. I towed it with our little Volkswagen to the Deer Park Caravan Park. The 'Jedda Country' band boys put up our annexe. They laid a floor and carpeted it. It was snug and neat. They often came over and had band practice in the annexe. They were a good bunch of guys, never too busy to help if needed.

Shelley and I got a job together, sorting fragmentised metal for Sims Metal. That was quite an experience for both of us. I enjoyed it and all the workers were female. The only male worker was the forklift driver but even some of the women operated the forklift. We started work at 5:00 am every morning and finished work at 2:00 pm.

This suited us fine, as most afternoons four of us from work would go for a spa and sauna in Yarraville before going home. We needed this because our job left us dirty and dusty. I think what I enjoyed the most about the job was that we all got on so well together and developed great friendships. We were always happy in each other's company and that made the workplace a pleasure to be in. A few of us worked weekends as well.

Some Saturday evenings I would go and listen to 'The Blue Echoes', another band that my brother was involved with. After his death they composed and recorded a song called, 'Friends' and dedicated it to him. Each time I went to see them they would have a table for me close to the stage and sing 'Friends' for me. I met Phil Golotta, the leader of the 'The Blue Echoes' and he introduced me to the band members. I always felt special, comfortable and at ease in their company, not only because they were Patrick's friends, but they treated me like I was one of them.

One Saturday night Phil picked me up and took me to the Bulleen Hotel where they were playing. At one stage he called me up on the stage, made an announcement that I was from New Zealand. He spoke of my brother and the song they had written for him then they sang it. Everyone stood up and clapped as Phil took me back to my table. I was aware that people were looking my way throughout the night, so I was a little uncomfortable. I didn't know anyone except Phil and was happy when it was time to go home. I have pleasant memories of times spent with many of Pat's friends, and they will always remain with me.

I experienced quite a few jobs when I came over to Australia and loved it because for the first fifteen of my working years I was school teaching and the only other work I knew was working as a fleeco in the shearing shed on my parent's property during the school holidays. That was fun too.

Anyway, Shelley moved on and took a job in Brunswick in a clothing factory where Rob Appleton, a friend of ours was the manager. I too moved on and started work as a barmaid in the Guiding Star Hotel on Geelong Road in Brooklyn. Greg Pitt was the manager. This was a hotel that catered mainly for interstate truck drivers. It opened at 6.00 am for breakfast and was always well patronised by truckies, early risers, and tenants from the Blue Moon Caravan Park across the road. While there, in 1982, I met and married Chris Toogood from St Albans, and we moved to a house in Essendon.

We adopted one of my granddaughters. Kerri-lee was eight months old when we moved into a shop in Ascot Vale that I had taken on. I sold giftware from New Zealand. It was called Kiwi Art and Crafts. I had a big Kiwi in the window. If it was a nice sunny day I would place the baby in her swing and put her out in front of the shop. I could see her from the counter. I remember an old couple who went walking every morning who would stop and chat with her. After a while, they would come into the shop and ask me if they could take her for a walk in her stroller. She was always asleep when they brought her back. Sometimes she'd have smudges of chocolate on her face.

I had the shop for a couple of years then gave it up as I wasn't getting any support from Chris and his drinking was too much for me to cope with. Our relationship became strained, and I moved back to 221 Pascoe Vale Road in North Essendon and worked in the St Kilda Inn in St Kilda. I took a contract cooking and running the dining room.

When my daughter Christine was sixteen years old she came over from New Zealand, and I had her and another Maori girl called June, working with me. They were great little workers and handled the dining room efficiently. The manager of the hotel was George Haenga, and he had Maori carvings put up on the walls of the public bar. When they were completed he invited the public to attend the unveiling of the carvings.

The mayor of St Kilda and his wife were the guests of honour. Also invited, was a very important Maori Elder from New Zealand. He came over to bless and unveil the carvings. There was a great attendance and there were sixteen baskets of hangi for the feast.

At that time, I had a small Maori Culture Group called 'Te Rangatahi', and they performed some Maori dance forms for the people who attended. The people here in Australia love the songs and dances of the Maori people of New Zealand.

After a couple of years, I moved on to Northcote with Kerri-Lee and got a job working for Nilsen's Sintered Products. I met a lot of people here from New Zealand so felt quite at home working there. This factory made metal products.

The Waves of Tangaroa

There are many kinds of waves
In the sea of Tangaroa
Big waves, little waves
High waves and low
Rolling, billowing
Curling, tumbling
Noisy waves, angry waves
Waves that toss
Waves that roar
And break as they come down.
Moody waves Rumbling waves
Crested waves
Foaming, frothing
White as snow
Riding on the breakers
Rippling, dancing
Sighing, running
To the shore
These are the saline salty waves
In the sea of Tangaroa, God of the sea.

Parked near the beach, enjoying the sea breeze as I watched the waves come ashore, I penned my thoughts about them.

I was there a while then moved with my granddaughter to a dual property in Messmate Street in Lalor. Kerri-Lee and I lived in the front house and my youngest daughter Christine and her partner and baby girl lived in the back house. That felt good to me.

Whilst there, I was asked by the police if I would be interested in working with young women under the umbrella of 'Winlaton Girls Institution' in Nunawading. They got to know of me through my involvement and work with troubled youth. I used to go to court with them, and also take them under my wing. So when they asked me I thought long and hard about it and agreed to take the position they offered me as 'Transitional Welfare Worker' for Winlaton. Kerri-Lee and I moved to a house supplied by the department in Nunawading when she was four years old. I had four, and sometimes five young women at a time living with us. My job was to prepare them for the transition from the institution back to the community. I found it quite challenging, yet rewarding.

I cared for twenty-four young women whilst there and saw them go from the institution; to me, then back to the community. This was really satisfying. Winlaton Women's Institution closed down after my five years with them.

If Only

If only it was possible to journey back in time
I'd wander back to yesteryear
when Nature was sublime
I'd tread the sacred pathways that my ancestors trod
They'd still be there to guide me to teach me
right from wrong.
To love and nurture Nature and all the elements
To walk with them and talk with them and listen to
their tales
As they sat around the campfire
at the closing of each day.
To hear their songs and chants of old,
about their men their warriors bold
Who fought in battles side by side
to keep the land they held with pride
Some did perish, a few survived
to tell the tales of those who died
So much is lost of our history
and will always remain a mystery.

I was penning my thoughts about going back in time
and having regrets about not being able to turn back
the hands of time and journey with my forebears
over their trails into the NOW.

BITS AND PIECES

Racism

I next moved to Fitzroy to be licensee and manager of a hotel for my nephew George Haenga.

Managing the hotel was quite a challenge for me as the majority of the clientele were aboriginal people. This hotel had been their drinking hole for thirty-six years. There were eight bar staff. Four on the morning shift, and four on the evening shift, each one having two days off a week. I got to know the aboriginal people well and found them interesting. I learned so much from them about their culture, and developed some great friendships.

I saw a lot of unfair treatment by the police to these people, with vivid memories of when the police raided the hotel. They brought mallets and dogs and smashed in doors. They took men and women into the toilets and searched them for drugs. Those who resisted were dragged out and thrown in police vans and taken away and locked up. They did not know who I was, so I was also stripped down to my knickers and bra, and my body was searched for needle holes. It was most embarrassing. Everyone in the hotel had been drinking and talking peacefully before the police arrived. I just couldn't believe what was happening.

When the police found out who I was, they were apologetic but by this time I was furious. However, the Liquor Commission made the police write me a letter of apology. The entire thing was wrong.

The newspaper came and interviewed me about the incident and took photographs. The story was on the front page of the local newspaper. The headlines read, *'Like something out of the Wild West'.* I have never forgotten how embarrassing it was. I understand why Aboriginal people feel bitterness towards the police because there were many incidents that I witnessed, where they have come into the hotel and deliberately hassled people who were quietly drinking. When they resisted they were dragged out to the waiting police vans parked outside the hotel.

I, as a Maori person, have had some experiences of a similar nature. I'm not sure if it's because of the colour of my skin but I can't help feeling that it was. I once walked into a shop and was the only one at the counter waiting to be served. The lady looked at me and continued to lean on the other end of the counter and totally ignored me, then another lady walked in, a white one, and the shop attendant immediately went over to serve her. The white lady told her that I was before her, and only then did she come and serve me. By then I was angry and walked out of her shop. It's not a nice feeling.

Some of my friends tell me I'm imagining it, but they have to have dark skin to know what we darkies experience in a white man's world. It's not right. We should be able to walk side by side and be treated as equals. Many times, we are looked down on when we don't deserve to be. I was married to an Australian, and he got angry when people stared at us being together. He'd ask them if I had something of theirs on and they would quickly look away. It was as if it was wrong for a white man to be with a dark skinned person. He has witnessed a lot of similar situations with me. It hurts. I believe that it has to change. I don't want my children, grandchildren and great grandchildren going through the same things because of the colour of their skin. I believe this behaviour goes back to the days when our respective countries were colonised by the English.

Even our inadequacies are always a perfect expression of life, a beloved child of the universe, a complete work of art, unique in all the world, so be happy, smile and keep on smiling.

Mystic Lady

Mystic lady, mystic lady
With eyes like an oasis in the desert
Deep pools of mystery
Saturated in history of your people
Gone on to the Dreamtime
They walk with you
They talk to you of mysteries
Unknown to us in our time
Ancestral guidance for the existence
and survival of your land and your people
Mystic lady, mystic lady
Servant of the Elders from the Dreamtime
Dream on mystic lady, dream on.

This poem is about an Aboriginal Elder, Lila Kirby, that I witnessed healing the sick at a Spiritual Gathering that I attended.

A FUNCTIONING MAORI SOCIETY

After colonisation, many things changed. I'm speaking now for my Maori people because when I look back over our history, life for the Maori people of New Zealand was simple. We had very close communities. Our people lived with nature and nature provided us with all our needs. Clothing was woven from plants such as the flax and kiekie. Warm cloaks and capes were made from the feathers of birds that roamed freely and inhabited the forests, such as the Kiwi, the Moa, the Kereru, the Weka, the Tui and a few others. The Moa and Huia have been extinct for many years, and the Kiwi is now protected by law.

The forest provided the Maori with berries and fruit from the trees, like the karaka, kotukutuku, titoki and kauka. Tawhara was a delicacy to the old people. This was jelly, which surrounded the stamens of the kiekie plant when it flowered. I remember going with my mother to the forest to get some for Pop when he was sick. There was a knack to taking the tawhara from the plant, as it was a plant that attached itself to the fork of another tree, and some of the trees were really tall. I used to watch my mother as she would take a long, thin pole with a v-shaped tip, and deftly thrust it up into the tree and twist the tops of the kiekie plant around the tip, then give it a quick jerk and it would break away from the tree. My job was to catch it as it came down. She would scrape out the jelly into a billy and repeat the process until she had enough to take home. When I look back over the years, I realise how much my mother taught me about the bounty that the forest provided us.

Meat was obtained from the forest; like the wild kunekune pig, the moa, the tui and the wood pigeon, especially when it was feeding on the Miro berry. So the forest was our source of supply as far as clothing and meat was concerned. Birds such as the tui and the pigeon were preserved in oil when they were plentiful. From the sea, fish was abundant. Mutton birds were a delicacy to the Maori.

Seasonal food was always dried or preserved to last for lean times and occasions, such as funerals and gatherings. There are very few today who still remember the old ways of our people. Our medicines were from the trees, plants, herbs and seaweed. We had our own Maori medicine men and women who studied and knew the medicinal value of the various plants and trees. Sadly, after colonisation most things changed for the Maori.

In the early 1800's, whalers and sealers came on their ships and they brought guns and other weapons. Many settled along the coasts of the north and south islands of New Zealand. We did not ask for them to be there.

Those who returned to England told of the lush country they 'discovered' and then began the mass migration of

English people. They brought with them their own belief systems and tried to wipe out ours. Their way of life that was totally alien to our people.

I truly believe that parenting has a lot to do with racism and that it all stems from way back then. They classed and treated the Maori people badly and called them uneducated, savage natives. These beliefs were handed on down through their generations and it still goes on today. It's sad but it's true. Only those who have lived and mingled with the Maori people know better. It's time to change all this and move forward as one.

We all need to teach our children how to live in harmony with all people, regardless of colour. They in turn can teach their children then the world will be a better place to live in. A world filled with harmony, love and caring for each other. That is the way it should be.

I have many white friends and I keep asking myself, why can't all other people be the same? One of the few places where I have been made to feel equal and accepted for who I am, is at the Spiritual Gatherings that I attend each year in different places around Australia. It's a beautiful feeling to be a part of these sacred gatherings, where the colour of your skin isn't an issue. This is a mix of young and old and some travel miles to be a part of this gathering.. Some come from different countries and it's just awesome to share stories and songs with each other around the sacred fire, at the meal table, and to learn about each other's culture and being respectful of each other. I am usually asked

Keep striving, keep moving forward because whatever we are facing at the moment will pass and we will move through it to whatever comes next.

The Melbourne Museum

The Museum, the treasure house stands proud.
The shelter and protector of the
sacred treasures of New Zealand
We greet and thank you for caring
and embracing these ancestral artefacts
To you, the handiworks of the forebears
Rest here in the warmth of this beautiful house
The proud boasts of your Maori people
Time destined you all to be here
to remain and be displayed
To the world and future generations to view
You will live on forever.

I wrote this poem when they transferred the Maori artefacts from the old Melbourne Museum to the new one to address the group, and always have plenty to say about their spiritual development, and cultural needs.

Respected elders are flown in from other countries and they bring with them inspiring stories, where they share of themselves and their culture so willingly. These sacred gatherings usually last for four days. Sometimes, for me personally, it all ends too soon but I go home energised and content. I always look forward to the next one.

So many memories flash through my mind as I write. I remember going back to 'Ratanui' each holiday when I was in my teens and my little brother Pat and I would wander to the creek down the bank below the homestead where I would feel under the willow tree roots for eels. Patrick would stand on the bank with a stick. When I felt an eel, his eyes would sparkle and he'd ask, "How big is it?" I'd indicate how round it was with my hands. "Two dongs for that one" he'd say. I'd pull it out and throw it on the bank. He would be so excited he would hit it mercilessly with his stick and wait for the next one. We spent hours, eeling up and down the creek, before taking our catch home. I couldn't eat them, but our neighbour Sid Haig loved eels, so he usually ended up with them.

Human beings are the most insane species. They worship an invisible God, and slaughter a visible nature, without realising that the nature they slaughter is the invisible God they worship.

Te Wiwi Piro

The putrid folk
from England
are bold
cunning
thieves
stenching our land
with its taxes, laws
and conditions
The stench of fish
and rotten crays
are pleasant odours
to the Maori
It's the Whiteman's stench
that is killing
all our pleasant
odours

QUINTEN

In the early 1990's I returned to New Zealand and was living in Pomare, a suburb north of Lower Hutt, New Zealand. My next door neighbours were Phil and Maria Taitua, who at that time had four sons. Andre, twins – Nathan and Gerald, and Troy, who became like grandsons to me. The twins used to wander over often to my garden and sit among the peas and help themselves. This family was very dear to me.

Maria was due to have another child, and I asked her to let me have the baby if it was a boy because she wanted a daughter. When the baby arrived, she decided to keep him. However, when he was two weeks old, Maria's mum passed away and she gave the baby to me to care for until she was ready to take him back. After two weeks, she came and took him home with her but he wouldn't settle. She rang me in panic, I asked her to bring him back to me. When she arrived, I took him and laid him down, and he quickly went to sleep. I asked her to go home and pack all his belongings and bring them over. She cried but agreed to leave him with me.

He was a gorgeous little baby boy and my family love him so much. His name is Quinten. He was a happy

One thing that I have learnt in my long life and that is to fight for what is right, fight for what you believe in, and fight for the ones you love. Never forget to tell someone how much they mean to you while they are alive.

contented baby and my family loved him then, and we all still love him now that he's grown up and making his own way in life.

When Quinten was three years old, we moved back to Australia, and my son Patrick came with us. We lived in a Melbourne suburb called Meadow Heights. Quinten went to Meadow Heights Primary School and was happy there. When he was nine years old, his mother came over for two weeks to spend time with him and asked if she could take him back to New Zealand for the Christmas holiday period. I was okay with that because I wanted him to know his birth family. By this time he had a sister and another brother. He went back to New Zealand with his mother and I never saw him again until he was twenty years old. I missed him so much and kept praying that he was okay.

I went back to New Zealand a year after he was taken to try to find him but when I knocked on the door of the home where they'd been living, a stranger answered and told me they had moved and didn't know where they were. My hopes of finding him seemed hopeless but I never gave up looking for him.

Years later, I was visiting my son in our home town Gisborne in New Zealand, when I called to see an old friend. While I was at her home, a young man walked in whom I recognised, although he was grown and was a handsome young man. I called his name. He spun around, looked at me, and said, "I remember you, you're Quinten's Nan." My heart skipped a beat and he came over and gave me a hug. My hopes of seeing my Quinten again seemed a real possibility. I asked him if he knew where he was and he told me where he lived. It all seemed too good to be true.

I immediately contacted my granddaughter Chelsea, who was on holiday in the area where Quinten was. A few days later she found him. She knew the street Quinten lived in, but not the street number, so she started door knocking at one end of the street and finally found him at the other end. She excitedly rang and told me, "I have found him."

He was twenty years old. I was so happy. On my way back to Melbourne l called in to see him. All the years of missing him were over. I was so happy to hold him close to me. My little boy had become a man. I spent the night with him and his parents and flew back to Melbourne the next day.

Miracles do happen. He came over to Australia a month later and my family and l were so happy to have him with us again. He started work two weeks later and is still here. I am so proud of the man he is. He has a beautiful partner, who is the love of his life, and together they are doing well here in the 'Land of the Dreamtime'.

MY THOUGHTS ON DEATH

I've thought a lot about death lately, after all, I am well into my eighties. I feel a deep peace within me and l don't fear death. I've lived a full life and when the time comes for me to leave this earthly plane I'll be ready. I see death as a graduation because l believe that we are all spiritual beings here on earth having a human experience, and when we've completed our mission here on earth, to the Creators satisfaction, we are returned to sender.

When I leave this place, I will be happy knowing my family are all well and coping in this ever changing world. I feel so blessed when I'm surrounded by them all. They've made my life worth living. I have no regrets.

You are the universe's offspring. Certainly no less than the trees, the moon or the stars. You have a right to be here.

Herbert Martin and I

POETRY

Poetry has been my passion since I was very young. I love writing about the beauty I see and feel in nature, the environment, the universe and the simplest things. I was not taught poetry, I felt it.

Five Generations

One day, one of my granddaughters phoned me to tell me about an American poetry competition. She wanted me to enter. "Why?" I asked. "For all the world", she said. So I did, and I won. I received a lovely big trophy.

Each day I would sit on my veranda to catch the morning sun and watch the rosebud as it grew in my front garden. I witnessed the development of a rose from its birth to its blooming, and this was the inspiration for my poem, 'The Rose' (elsewhere in the book).

When Kiri was awarded her poetry prize, she became good friends with Herbert Woodward Martin. Herbert is a poet of renown, and taught at the University of Dayton where he taught creative writing and African American Literature. .

About Kiri's Poetry

'The Rose' was featured as the first poem in the book of the International Society of Poetry book. It offered the following Artist's Profile: Kiri Atawhai Dewes, Melbourne, Australia.

Other poems with awards are: A Better Place; A Dew Drop and The Humpback Whale.

A few of her poems are in the NZ schooling system, and educational poetry books, for English and Maori.

Kiri was awarded the Editors Choice for the International Society of Poets for five years running. In the 2005 edition *Twilight Musings*. She also had a poem selected to be the very first in their book, *Timeless Voices* with The Humpback Whale.

Three things that cannot be hidden – the sun,
the moon, and the truth.

A Fire

There's a fire burning brightly
Deep within my heart
Pulsing, aching
Is my love
for you, my beloved
Don't you ever turn away
Let us be as one
Lest the flame expires
Within this heart of mine.
In my deepest reverie
In my every dream
Visions of you haunt me
Night and day and always
You are my obsession
You're my every dream
You keep the fire burning
Within this heart of mine.

I was asked to write a poem about a fire. I wrote of the fire burning in my heart.

www.ingramcontent.com/pod-product-compliance
Lightning Source LLC
Chambersburg PA
CBHW050313010526
44107CB00055B/2218